THE KEYS TO SUCCESS

For Everyday People

By Christopher Williams

iUniverse, Inc.
Bloomington

The Keys to Success
For Everyday People

iUniverse books may be ordered through booksellers or by contacting:

iUniverse
1663 Liberty Drive
Bloomington, IN 47403
www.iuniverse.com
1-800-Authors (1-800-288-4677)

ISBN: 978-1-4759-4251-4 (sc)
ISBN: 978-1-4759-4252-1 (e)

Library of Congress Control Number: 2012916877

Printed in the United States of America

iUniverse rev. date: 12/7/2012

DEDICATION

This book is dedicated to my mother Mary Williams and my father, the late Elder Jimmie Lee Williams, Sr. Thank you for being a guiding light. Your work ethics, dedication, and determination lives in me. In addition, this book is dedicated to my beautiful wife and kids. Today we face a big world, and you will need to know how to succeed.

CONTENTS

FOREWORD

By: Billy Brown II

I AM EXCITED TO have brought a person of such great caliber into my life by the name of Chris Williams who wrote this book Keys to Success that outlines the principals to promote achieving success.

As I read the work, it became very clear that the keys can be applied to everyday life and is something that every person, no matter your history, race, sex, or religion, can apply them today for immediate improvement on your quality of life.

For massive change in your life, would you go to your neighbor who is sitting on the porch or someone that is living what he writes about. In this book, Chris takes us to the level that he is living in his life at this very moment and is having such success in his business, personal, and spiritual life.

A chapter that stood out to me was the one titled Thinking like a Winner; it is true the way you think leads to your actions and outcomes in life. As I travel the United States speaking in front of thousands of people each year, it is clear that we become what we think. The book follows this with a statement of "successful people are action people" which shows us that in order to obtain a goal or anything in life you have to take action today to obtain it and stop putting it off.

The book outlines some major points that apply to why we have the problems in our life and our country today. We have a value problem that we can correct with the steps outlined in the book. Faith, mind set, attitude, focus and money management followed up with giving to others which ties everything together under Luke 6:38 "Give and it will be given to you" NIV

I know that when you apply the keys given within this book your life will change for the good and you will affect many people around you to make this a better world.

Billy J Brown II

Author, Motivational Speaker

Introduction

For many years, I worked very hard, but I was only able to achieve a low level of success. After several failed business ventures, I pondered what it took to achieve success. After finishing nursing school in 1996, I worked and ran a part-time lawn service business. Whenever possible I took additional training in business courses and consulted with successful business owners concerning success. My awakening moment was after my father suddenly took ill and passed away in 1997. Even though I had opened businesses before, I finally realized that life was short and you should take action on things you wanted to do. I realized that you do not get a practice life and that time is precious. This helped me overcome some fears in regards to success. In 2001, I started an Assisted Living Facility and transitioned to a Certified Residential Facility in 2002.

Often, people would ask me what it takes to be successful. I realized that most people indeed want to succeed, but they simply do not know how. How you become successful is not something people typically discuss on a regular basis. Many people think it is a secret or simply luck. This is far from the truth.

The Keys to Success convey general principles that will help the reader understand what is required to achieve success. These principles are simplified so everyday people can understand them. You will be given general biblical references concerning some principles to solidify their validity. Once you have read this book, the keys to success should be applied daily to get the maximum results. Results will vary depending upon your determination and actions.

In the early chapters in this book, some views and myths on success will be discussed. The keys to success looks at having the right mind frame is critical to success. This book will provide techniques to assist in getting in the right mind frame for success. This includes setting goals, combating fears, and eliminating procrastination. Once success is obtained, this book gives principles on maintaining success through money management and giving.

SUCCESS

WHAT DO YOU THINK about being successful? What does being successful mean to you? Do it even matter to you? First, let us discover a general meaning of success. To some extent, success means an achievement of something planned, desired, or attempted. For some, success could even mean gaining fame or prosperity. The meaning of success depends on your individual views, plans, and desires. The definition of success by Ralph Waldo Emerson is described as the following: to laugh much; to win respect of intelligent persons and affection of children; to earn approbation of honest critics and endure the betrayal of false friends; to appreciate beauty; to find the best in others; to give of one's self; to leave the world a little better, whether by a healthy child, a garden patch, or a redeemed social condition; to have played and laughed with enthusiasm, and sung with exultation; to know even one life has breathed easier because you have lived; this is to have succeeded. As you can see, there are many ways to describe success. Again, the true definition of success will be determined by you. To be successful, you definitely need to be able to recognize what you are trying to achieve to know when you have arrived at that point. For starters, you simply have to want to be successful to even consider obtaining success.

In today's society, there are many avenues available to become successful. Even though there are many roads that can lead to success, there are only a few simple key ingredients that propel someone to obtaining success. No matter what your goals are in life, you must learn to adopt practices to obtain success. It would be great if you could master these practices at a very young age, but most people do not. Some people never do. Do not worry, you can start learning and utilizing these practices today. No matter what point you are in life, if you master these principles, you will be successful.

Let's begin at the finish line or at the end. Let's imagine you are already successful. Picture yourself at whatever state of success you desire. Would you be a millionaire? If you ask most Americans what their financial goal is, many would say to become a millionaire. In many ways, society is fixated on obtaining a million dollars. There are even game shows and contests that lure us into thinking we could win a million dollars. The lottery and casinos make millions of dollars off people trying to obtain a million dollars. What if you did actually win. What if you were a millionaire. What would you do with the money? Would you buy that luxury home or car you have always wanted? Maybe you could pay off some bills or take an exotic vacation to anywhere in the world. At some point, we have all thought about what it would be like if we could spend without the worry of bills and running out of money. Believe it or not, this is the reality for many everyday people. Many people amongst you have achieved their dream of becoming a millionaire. The next everyday millionaire could be you! Most millionaires did not obtain their money from playing sports, entertainment, inheritance, lawsuits nor by playing the lottery. When I found this out in my late teens, I was very surprised. This was hard to believe because of the media's obsession with the wealth and material possessions of entertainers. We see luxury mansions on MTV cribs and we assume most rich people must play sports or work in entertainment. These individuals are a small percentage of rich Americans. Most people become a millionaire through business, sales, investments, and real estate. Even though many succeed in these areas, it is not these actual areas that make them successful. Now you are probably wondering if it is not a certain field of study, what it could be. It is the key principles these individuals apply in order to become successful. These same principles are used by athletes, entertainers, etc. Knowing these principles, highly successful people share common views and characteristics pertaining to success. This is not a gimmick or a get rich quick scheme. These are real practices that get real results! If you are looking to get rich over night, do not read this book; just go buy a lottery ticket. If you are seeking to become successful to the fullest, this is for you. Of course, you will learn practices that can make you lots of money, but this is not for someone seeking get rich quick schemes.

Now, let us go back to the beginning. I read an internet blog concerning two homeless brothers that lived in a Budapest cave that found out they were the beneficiaries of their grandmother's 4 billion dollars. Yes, 4 billion dollars! That is a lot of zeros. A family friend spent months trying to locate the brothers to inform them of their fortune. I am sure this family friend was rewarded for locating the two brothers. He followed a road map to locate the brothers, which resulted in a few million dollars. Following the road map is definitely the key.

Could you imagine someone locating you like the brothers in the cave? It would be great to find out there was a large sum of money you had to claim for no apparent reason. In a sense, you do have money and other items to claim. In life, your success is laid up for you to go get it. What if you found out that an account was opened fifty years ago by a relative and you are the sole beneficiary of a million dollars. Would you go claim it? This would be life changing! Could you use the money immediately? The only catch to this is you must travel to a foreign country to find a safe deposit box that contains information concerning where to collect your money. Does this still sound exciting? This is how life is. Will you go claim what is rightfully yours or will you simply give up on it?

To claim your inheritance, the benefactor specifically states you must locate the safe deposit box alone. Once you get the instructions, you realize that no one in the foreign country speaks your language. Before you give up, a final notation indicates that your relative did leave you a road map in your language and the keys to the safe deposit box to help guide you along the way. Now, the question is do you think you can follow the steps to get to the reward? This is an odd scenario, but this represents the obstacles we face in life in order to get to where we are trying to go. Just as you face opposition in the scenario, life will have obstacles seen and unseen that you will face on the road to becoming successful. All will face the obstacles of life, so it only makes sense to stick to the road map. Will you stick to the road map? Will you take hold of the keys to success? Successful individuals always follow the road map. If you wanted to bake a cake, it would be smart to follow the instructions on the back of the box. If you are a scholar, this is really how the scientific method operates. If you follow the instructions, you should get the same results that others did. This opens the door to conquer many things if you are willing to follow. You have just taken the limits off everything. This should let you know that all things are possible.

Some people think success just happens. This is untrue. Some people may even think success just happens to certain people. This is also not true. Success is simply up to each individual. Yes, it is simply up to you. You are probably thinking if success is up to an individual, why someone would not want to be successful. It is not that someone does not want to be successful. Most people really do desire success. The problem is most people are not following any road maps to become successful. They simply do not know how to become successful. Many people go through life just trying to wing it and hope for the best. Their hope is, maybe one day they will be successful. Maybe one day! One day comes every single day. That one day could be today! It is time to walk in your destiny. This is your road map. The good thing about following the road map is, you will know where you are at all times when you follow the road map.

In my research, I have found similar traits in all highly successful people. I began to use these traits everyday and I saw a significant difference in my outcomes. I have been to many seminars, read hundreds of books and articles, listened to numerous audio series, etc. After listening to all the Tony Robbins, the Donald Trump's, the Sam Walton's, the Zig Ziglar's, and the Robert Kiyosaki's of the world, I realized that there were some common things they all were saying. All of these keys or principles were associated with highly successful people. They were so plain and simple, I almost thought it couldn't be true. After finding out these things, I wanted to tell just about anyone who would listen to me. I felt like even though the information was out there, no one really shared it openly. Often, I came across individuals that did not know this information was available. I have learned that many people are at poverty level simply due to not having knowledge or the know how to get out. Again, in my encounters, many people simply did not know these success practices existed. Whenever used, these simple practices can be life changing. Just imagine if you used them, but did not become as successful as a Donald Trump did. Even then, you definitely would be in good company. Any improvement would be an increase. In this book, you will learn the keys to success. This is your road map to your treasure that has eluded you for too long. Many people have followed this road map before you, so do not be afraid. As you read this book, be open minded and become highly successful.

What does it take to be successful? Think about this for a moment. Now think about why some people succeed and others don't? Are they smarter than you are? Is it because they are just simply better than you are? Let us be honest, we often question ourselves concerning this when it comes to achieving. This question puzzles many people. We have all tried to achieve something at some point and did not. In our minds, we evaluate ourselves and wonder what went wrong. Many scholars have come up with many theories concerning why some succeed and others fail. Many theorists concentrate only on scientific measures and factors concerning why people fail. To get a total understanding, I will not only use information gained from scholars, but a few biblical references as well. This will give you a deeper understanding about success and its principles.

If you are already successful, this book will promote and revisit things you currently practice. In addition, it will encourage increased growth and development. You can be successful on a level that you have never imagined. One thing for sure, God has no respect of person in regards to success. This is only saying that if someone else can be successful, so can you. Knowing this, the next successful person you know, should be you. I used to think, people that were highly successful were sort of a different kind of human being or something. In my mind, it just seemed like successful people had everything together all the time. I would even question myself concerning what was the difference in them and me. This is not uncommon for someone to compare one's self to the images we see portrayed as successful on television, in magazines, etc. Even though we should never let society paint a picture for us concerning what success is, we sometimes make comparisons. Remember, success is individualized, but I did not know that at the time.

Growing up, I felt like I was just as deserving to be successful as anyone else, which was the right way to think. I would work very hard and always gave my very best, but I often ended up with average or just above average results. This really bothered me. At a very young age, I was a big sports fan. My favorite sport was basketball. I started playing Junior Varsity basketball and moved up to the Varsity team in my freshman year of high school. I ran the miles, took hundreds of shots a day, and got the grades. I worked very hard and often wondered why I did not make it to the professional level. I wondered why some of the guys I played with didn't make it further. Of course, there was more than just one factor, but no matter what, we look back over our life and wonder why something did not work out for us. As most young people, I idolized people I saw in the spotlight that I thought were successful. We see these individuals in magazines and on television each day. I felt within, I could be just like them, but often I fell short. This really bothered me because I really wanted to succeed at a high level as I had imagined. What is it, I would wonder. What is it that allows someone to succeed and others don't? I remember times actually crying due to my dissatisfaction with my level of achievement. I would look at certain actors and I thought to myself maybe it is the look. They look better than everyone else does. Guess what, it is not how you look. Your looks do not have anything to do with it. You can be fat, skinny, tall, short, bald, blind, black, white, or purple. The factors that we make so big in our minds are not the things that stop us from being highly successful. Gabourey Sidibe, better known for her role in "Precious", is obviously overweight. Her weight has not stopped her from achieving a high level of success. These things have little to do with anything. I recall reading an article concerning Danny DeVito's story at a young age. Nothing against Danny DeVito, but this really confirmed to me it could not be the looks. What I did notice in his story was how he was determined to follow his dreams. Danny DeVito was a hairdresser / barber before leaving it all to follow his dreams of becoming a movie star. His story was very inspirational and confirmed to me that an ordinary person can achieve extraordinary things. I did not want to become an actor, but I knew there had to be some common traits among successful people and it was not the looks.

I wondered constantly what separated the wanna – be from the super achiever. I knew at this point it wasn't looks so maybe it was smarts. It has to be intelligence! Then I read many stories and heard testament about people who did not finish high school or college, but were highly successful. I heard about Bill Gates who dropped out of college and later became the richest man in the world. We all know someone personally who did not finish high school, but was able to have a successful life. Do not get me wrong, knowledge and education is always important. Knowledge is very powerful, but it does not guarantee your success. There are millions of people with an education, but they are not highly successful. For example, you could be a Physician and still have bad credit or be broke. Yes, a Physician has an enormous amount of education, but if you're a broke Physician, are you really educated…… Even though education is important, I realized it wasn't the single key to becoming highly successful. Education is definitely a key to achieving success, but it is not the only key. We will talk about education and knowledge later in this book.

The more answers I would find concerning success, it seemed like the more questions I would think of. Surely, I knew at this point, there wasn't one single thing that propelled you to success. I remember praying and asking God, what is it? What is it, that successful individuals have that I do not. I wanted to know why I was not achieving even though I tried very hard and always worked so hard. I was disgusted and hated getting mediocre results. I wanted to achieve more than just average results. I felt like why bother to go to work if you are working just to be broke. I continued to work, but felt like I could stay home and do that. I know we have been taught not to question God, but I wanted to know. I cried and prayed for an answer for days. After several days, the answer came to me very plain and simple. It was so plain until I thought it should have been more complex. I knew the answer was right because this was a bridge I had never crossed before. Indeed, it was not about looks or just having smarts. It is all about renewing your mind. Renew my mind! This sounded just too plain to me. Furthermore, you have to deprogram your mind from your mediocre thought process and develop a new way of thinking at that point. Now I was wondering what does this have to do with anything. What did this have to do with being successful? This is very critical to becoming highly successful!

Did you know your mind is where success starts? Highly successful people think different from mediocre folks. Their way of thinking is totally different. Did you know whatever is produced in the natural occurs in the supernatural first? This is referring again to your mind. All things that evolve to the physical are birthed and perceived in the mind first. It is not that the super achievers are better than you are; their outlook is always above average results. Their mindset is programmed to do more and expect more than average. They always go beyond what the average go. They work harder and do more than the average. They step outside of their comfort zone even if they have deficiencies or weaknesses. I realized, with this new mind frame there would be no limits if someone faced their weaknesses instead of running from their weaknesses. I realized I did not have to take no for an answer with this new mind. Just imagine if you never took no for an answer when trying to succeed at anything. If the bank tell you no, your new attitude is, what do I need to improve because I am coming back. Now that you know all of this, success is truly up to you. I realized that if I went beyond that place of mediocrity, it would be no way I could fail. I immediately bought into the concept that it was totally up to me. I know we have all heard that before, but it is true. Your success is up to you. It is God's will for us to succeed. We must be willing to condition our minds or to simply renew it to think in a new way.

Realize that the super achievers are people just like you and I. We know at this point that one of the differences is, they have changed their mind frame and they go the extra mile every single time. Think about a professional athlete that trains repeatedly at a certain sport over and over again until it is mastered. Just think about how the basketball phenom Lebron James trains daily even in the off-season. I remember meeting Lisa Leslie, from the WNBA in the off-season before she retired, while working out at a gym. She was running and working out as if she had a game the next week. I thought within myself, she is on vacation and she is still driven. That same year she stood out amongst her peers in the WNBA. She was better prepared and got better results. Highly successful people get better results because of their focus in a particular area or subject for long periods of time. Think about it, if you shoot 1,000 jump shoots a day for five years, don't you think your jump shot would improve. Of course it would! Think about a young woman who just got married that cannot cook biscuits. Her first patch of homemade biscuits may be hard as a brick and only good to knock out a burglar. After twenty years, they still may be hard as a brick. Just kidding! Indeed, after that long, she will be a master at cooking biscuits after all the repeated attempts. We learn and master things by repetition. When we do something over and over again, we master it. We are surprised when we can sing a song after hearing it over and over. After learning these keys to success, they should be studied and applied over and over to achieve high success.

Highly successful people always go beyond the average when mastering skills. They work harder, study harder, work longer, and study longer. Believe it or not, they start off at the same point as most of us, but they always go beyond. Some say we all start off on an equal playing field, but we know this is not true in every circumstance. We know some people are born into wealth and some into poverty. For the most part, most people are not born into wealth. Most people are born way below being rich. By knowing this, one should say to him or herself, "All successful people are human just like me. " Just know if they can do it, so can you. Believe me; they had to start from somewhere. You would be surprised that many successful people started worst then you. It is not about how you start but how you finish.

Most highly successful people go from the very bottom to the top. Some might simply say, they have gone from rags to riches. Something occurs along the way that make achievers get sick and tired of being sick and tired. Something clicks in their mind to make them take on a new way of thinking. This is called an awakening. You have to wake up and develop a new way of thinking. Once you decide to accept this new way of thinking, you must fight to stay at that level of thinking because doubt is always nearby. In this book, you are going to learn what it takes. After getting in the right mind frame, you must believe that you can achieve anything at a higher level than you have ever dreamed of. Do not forget, it is simply up to you! Basically, it is how bad do you want it. Do you really want it? Do you want it bad enough that you will change your thinking and take action?

This is a self-help book that should be used as a guide. This is a tool for you on your journey to achieve success or a level of greater success. After learning these principles, you should utilize them daily. You will see improvements and get better results. You have taken the first step by opening the book. A lot of things may be going through your mind concerning success at this point. Most of these keys to success are very simple, but they must be applied. It is time that you really let it all sink in and apply it in your daily life. It is your time to go higher! If you are currently successful, it is time to spread your wings to become even more successful. Whatever point of success or failure you are, if you do the same thing this year that you did last year, you will get the same results. Albert Einstein said, "To do the same thing over and over and expect a different result is insane." Think about it that way, if you have tried something your way and it failed, wouldn't it make sense to try it another way. Again, it is time to go beyond your old ways of thinking about success.

What Is Success To You

WHAT IS SUCCESS? I said earlier that success was the achievement of something desired, planned, or attempted. It is a point in one's life when a higher point is achieved in anything that exceeded mediocrity or your expectations. Notice, it should exceed your expectations. Knowing this, your success is not determined by how others feel. It is how you feel. True success is when you have a sense of fulfillment. First, you must define what being successful is to you. Success is approved by the individual that is experiencing it. This is also a part of getting into the right mind frame. From this day forward, know that no one determines whether you have reached the point of being successful but you. The reason is that society discriminates when it chooses what is acceptable or represents success. When we focus on what society say being successful is, we tend to focus only on our shortcomings. For example, society promotes women who are tall, blonde, and thin as being the ideal appearance of an attractive woman. If a woman bases this on how she should look, she may not feel that she is as appealing if she does not fit that description. No matter what your appearance is, you are unique. You can only be you and trying to be someone else is not being true to yourself. Tell yourself that you are not less than anyone else is. That is right, no one is better than you are. Society sometimes tells us that money or success brings true happiness. Money and success will not bring true happiness. Being happy is a quality of successful people, but true success involves fulfillment. Again, do not let anyone define your meaning of success but you. You and not outside sources should determine success in every area of your life.

It should never be determined by what you view from media outlets. Of course, nothing is wrong with a thin pretty blonde woman, but you are reprogramming your way of thinking. You are starting to take back control of your mind. As you continue to reprogram your mind, you will continue to gain the tools to succeed and shape your desired outlook towards success.

At this point, we know that we determine what success is, but at what point are we successful. Some people compare themselves or seek approval from others to judge what they have achieved. Remember not to base what someone else thinks is your success or not. This is based on how you feel. Some people achieve many things, but feel empty. There could be many reasons for this, but just know that outside influences should never be a reason. What you call success may not mean anything to the next person. That is why we must lose sight on what others think concerning what success means to us. You can be a janitor and someone may say, you are not successful because you are only a janitor. If being a janitor is higher than what you were or thought you could be, then you are a successful janitor. If this was a higher step than what you were, then you have experienced growth. Being successful is not about a title. You can have a title and not have a dime in your pocket. Again, being successful is not always about having lots of money either. The reason it is not simply about money is that we know that money cannot buy you happiness. In addition, you can make plenty of money and be in debt. This is where many people go wrong. They think if I make a lot of money, I will not have any problems. I repeat, true success is about fulfillment. Success is about productivity and management. That is why you could be a janitor and still be successful. Sometimes we look at a person and say that they are only this or that, but that might be a step up if they came from less. A lot of times, we focus on what we are not instead of being thankful from which we came and what we are. Some people let others make them feel low due to having a so-called low title or ranking. We make a title larger than it really is. I have personally known Licensed Practical Nurses or Licensed Vocational

Nurses that make more money than Registered Nurses do. Some Registered Nurses make money more than some Physicians. A title does not mean someone is successful or not. There are some doctors that are broke just like poor people. Knowing this, a title is just a description of an individual's job. It does not mean someone is greater or less than someone else is. Once you develop the mindset that success is how you feel about your state in life, achieving more will come easier. Now is the time to get in the mind frame of successful thinking and reach your highest potential.

God truly wants you to be successful and have a more abundant life. He will bless you for simply stepping out on faith and removing that old limited way of thinking. You could be so blessed that your cup runs over. Now that is enough to even bless others. I have a constant expectation! I am constantly looking for my overflow of blessings. I have an expectancy of being successful. Program your mind to always expect positive things to come your way. You must learn to think in this way at all times. Have you ever poured soda in a glass and the suds began to over flow? This is the type of expectancy you should have when it comes to success. Remember, you cannot think mediocre anymore. Tell yourself that your suds are about to over flow. It happens so quickly that it over flows on everything around it. When you experience success, it will touch everything around you. You will be able to help others in many ways. God is good to us all no matter who we are. He rains on the just and the unjust. This means that it does not matter how good you are or how bad you are. If you have faith and believe you can achieve something, you can.

In today's society, things are quickly changing. Things change at such a fast pace that the future is now. We must prepare, be aware, and make good decisions due to so many uncertainties. Years ago, you could count on finding a job immediately after finishing high school. Today things are very different. Today, you must have some sort of trade, a college education, or some form of training just to make an average wage. Even after all of that, there may not even be a job waiting for you. People use to work and look forward to retirement, but now people are retiring yet to return back to work. In this forever-changing society, you must plan ahead. We can no longer count on our employers to set things up for our future. Many people have learned too late that they should have been more involved in their own life. In this new way of thinking, take an active role in your own life by making the tough decisions for your future. Who knows what you want for the future better than you do? Who would work harder for you to obtain that future harder than you would? As you continue to gain the keys to success, take an active approach and plan ahead today.

Do You Desire Success?

THIS IS A QUESTION you must seriously ask yourself. Well do you really want to be successful? Think about it sincerely. Are you really trying to reach your goal(s) that you have been contemplating for so long? If you truly want to be successful, just do it. I know you are thinking that it is easier said than done, but it is just that simple. Nike, Inc. coined a phrase in the 1980's, "just do it". Well, if you really want it, the slogan makes you immediately think about taking some sort of action. Now ask yourself, what are you doing to help reach your goals? Your answer to this will reflect your seriousness towards achieving your goals. To make it even more urgent, what have you done today to propel you towards your dream or goal? When you think about it, many people start working towards something, and after so long, they quit. There are plenty of people talking about success, but doing little to reach it. Just do it! To be highly successful, your dream must become your daily life. Dress like it! Talk like it! You should do something every single day to work towards reaching your goals. Remember, as I mentioned earlier Lisa Leslie worked out excessively the year she excelled and won a WNBA championship. Every day we should do something to move towards our goal. Lisa Leslie worked out everyday, which helped her reach her goal. If you did this, you would get closer and closer to your dream. Now, if I ask again if you want to be successful, you can see that you can do more than what you are already doing. By making this observation, let it sink in your mind that indeed, success is up to you and you're going to do more each day, each hour, each minute, each second, etc. By doing this, your goal(s) will become your passion. You become driven everyday to do something towards your dream, which becomes your love and passion.

Now that you know that you can do and give more than what you have given, ask yourself what your dreams are. Determine what exactly your goal(s) or dream(s) are. The next question is, how long have they been just that, dreams and goals? Are you closer today than you were yesterday? Are you one of those people still waiting for one day? For some people one day will never come. As I said earlier, one day comes every day. Some things are closer within our reach than what we know. Often we focus on others as if they have the power or control over everything, but no one plays a bigger part in your destiny than you. Even though others will influence us, we are the ultimate decision maker. The decisions you make today will determine your tomorrow. This is true when trying to do or become anything. That is why I asked, what you are doing each day to reach your goals.

At this point, you should have realized that success do not come easy or by luck. Although the keys to success are simple, success is earned. Most people want things handed to them, but something easily obtained is not valued compared to something worked for. Develop the attitude that no one owes you anything. Quite frankly, no one does! From this day forward, have the attitude that you will not wait for someone else to do the things you can be doing for yourself. This promotes action! Why put off what you could do today for tomorrow. Tomorrow will have its own new tasks, problems, and situations. When you fully develop this attitude, you will stay driven and take an active approach towards everything. This is the right attitude you should maintain this day forward.

Some people think highly successful people do less, but they actually do more than the average. It may appear that they do less, but they have mastered taking action, multi-tasking, and getting quicker results. Again, learning by repetition works! If you do something constantly or for long periods of time, you will master it. When situations arise, successful individuals take immediate action and resolve things immediately. By doing this, they are able to solve more problems. When you are able to solve more problems and get more tasks done, you will increase your results. When you increase your results, you increase your benefits. If people had the mindset of an ant that blocks out complaining and take immediate action on tasks, the world would be a better place. Block negative thoughts out of your mind. Block it out of your mind that you are going to wait on someone else to do something or to help you become successful. Have the attitude that if you are not helping yourself, why should someone else help you. Do not get this confused with delegating tasks and utilizing experts. The key is to simply take action. Do not be hindered by someone else's lack of passion and desire. When others see that you are giving 100%, they are more prone to help you. You must believe in what your own dream is before people can believe in your dream. The way you show others you believe in it is, do something every single day. Have you heard people say I am going to do this as soon as …! You can feel in the blank. The fact remains, we do not bulge because their non-action shows that they do not believe in what they are saying. I remember when I was 20 years old and I applied for a business loan at a large banking institution. I was asking for a whopping $100,000 loan. The banker asked me how much of my own money was I planning to use toward this business. I told him that I was going to use the money I had in my account. He checked my account I had with them, and I had $800 in it. He told me to put myself in his shoes. Would I be willing to sponsor someone financially on a venture if he or she had almost nothing to invest? He went on to explain that if I did not help myself, others would not be willing to help. Therefore, being successful is more than just talk and relying on others. It is about just doing it and by taking action yourself.

Major success is obtainable for everyday people just like you. Sometimes we make our goals seem too big and distant in our own minds until they seem unreachable. We often accept doubtful thinking that we are not good enough or smart enough. You have to picture yourself as being successful before it even happens. This is sort of like saying; I can see myself in four years completing that degree, etc. You must visualize it first! The bible even tells us that faith is the substance of things hoped for, the evidence of things not seen. Even though you do not physically see it, you have to visualize it. You have to see it in your mind. Picture yourself at the point you desire. If you can see it, you can be it. On the other hand, if you cannot see it, you cannot become it. This is a part of getting in the right frame of mind. Everything that happens outward starts inward. All of your goals and dreams must occur first in your mind before they can occur outside of your mind. The simple fact is, you must see yourself as being successful in whatever to stay driven to reach your goal. The right mindset is very powerful and critical to success.

Once there was a young woman that wanted to pursue a career in singing. She had a beautiful voice and the support of her family. At the age of 19, she became pregnant out of wedlock and was very doubtful of accomplishing her dream of having a professional singing career. After having her daughter Zion, she got very little support from the father of her child. Even though she knew she had a hard road up ahead, she did not hold her head down. She continued to raise her daughter and follow her dream of singing. She sang at her parent's church, but always had bigger dreams. She entered into a contest against 70,000 other contestants. Yes, that is correct 70,000 contestants nationwide! Against all odds, Fantasia Burrino topped all singers to become an American Idol in 2004. Fantasia believed it could happen for her before it happen. Again, if you cannot picture it, you might as well not try. Have you ever been around someone that voices, "I knew I was going to lose". If you knew it, why even show up! Fantasia could have said within herself, I have no chance with all these people auditioning around the country. Instead, she believed it could be. You must believe that it could be you. No matter how big the obstacles may seem, it can be done. It is going to happen for somebody, so why not you.

WORTHY OF SUCCESS

I THINK THAT YOU deserve to obtain success and live life to the fullest. The question is, do you feel this way? Do you deserve to be successful? The answer to this question is very important. You have learned that no one is better or more deserving than you are. You are just as deserving to be successful as the next person. Even though I am telling you this, you must believe you are worthy to be successful. It is important for you to know that you are deserving. If you do not feel like you are deserving of good things, you will not strive to obtain good things. It does not matter how long you have been at the bottom, you are worthy of obtaining success. You got to believe this! There maybe times you feel like you are not the smartest, your just winging it, or you are just going through the motion. Guess what, successful people often feel this way at times. The fact is, successful individuals do not let these doubts stop their productivity. Again, you are no different from the next person. You are no different from Bill Gates, Shaquille O'Neal, or Oprah. Well, you are a little different, but my point is that they are human just like you and I. They put their socks on one foot at a time just as you do. Well, Oprah stylist put her socks on one at a time, but you get the point. Believe it or not, some of them started off worse than you. Just know that you can be the first in your family to achieve great success. You are deserving of achieving success no matter what your background and experience may or may not be. Do not worry if your family has a history of failure. Use those failures as teaching tools to avoid failures.

Having a belief that you are worthy to be successful promotes you taking action, a positive outlook, and the development of the right mind frame. Not believing you are worthy promotes doubt, procrastination, and fear. Always have the mindset that you are worthy to be at the top in life. It does not matter if someone else thinks you do not deserve. Your positive outlook will help you avoid all negative energy. Close your eyes and meditate saying I am worthy and I am successful. Do this exercise periodically. Indeed, you are worthy to be successful. You must simply believe you are no matter what. Everybody has a story or come from something. Do not let depression or circumstances hinder your future of success.

Is Abundance Bad?

THERE ARE MANY BIBLE passages that let us know that God wants us to be blessed. It further lets us know we can be blessed in an abundant way. So if this is true, why do some people make others feel like having abundance is a bad thing? Is it because of ignorance, jealousy, or something else? Let us take a closer look at this. The bible lets us know that Job was the richest man in the East. It also talked about kings and their riches. So if we know that there were many men of the bible whom were prosperous, why can't we be? Of course, the bible asks the question, "What does it profit a man to gain the whole world and lose his soul?" Does this mean profiting is bad? This biblical passage does not say abundance is bad. Clearly, this states that our soul is more important than profiting many riches. Knowing this, our priorities should always be in order. God should always be number one in our lives and in every area, including over financial gain. We must remain mindful not to make money or material items more valuable to us than God. It is the way we look at things in our heart.

Have you ever heard the one about money being evil or the route to all evil? "Money is the route to all evil", is a frequent saying we hear often when talking about money or being prosperous. This saying had me puzzled for many years. I wondered why God would want us to be blessed and then say it was evil. Did God really say or mean that? This really did not make sense to me. I decided to find this scripture and read it for clarity for myself. After reading the scripture a few times, I understood it very clearly. I realized that people left off the most important part of the verse. The scripture actually says, "For the love of money is the route to all evil." By just adding the missing text gave the scripture a completely new meaning. I realized that I had been hearing an incomplete phrase for years from people who probably did not know the true meaning themselves. For the love of money, that would definitely be the route to all evil. Now, this time, it made plenty of sense. Of course, for the love of money people do all sorts of evil deeds. People will steal, sell drugs and their body, lies, and kills just to obtain money. This made sense, because God certainly would not bless us abundantly to promote evil. So having money is not a bad thing. For the love of it, people do many evils acts trying to obtain it. Lack of money, often tempt many individuals to possess it wrongly. The bible actually says that money is the answer to all things. So know that trying to achieve is not a bad thing. God actually wants you to prosper in an abundant way.

What Did Others Do To Be Successful

You have answered yes to the question, do you want to be successful. Now, what is the fastest and easiest way to become successful? The answer is to simply do what other successful people are doing. Want to be unsuccessful? Simply do what unsuccessful people are doing. It is really that simple. Find out what successful people are doing to achieve success and follow it. Once you establish what you want to do, find a mentor. You can have several mentors if you like. Once you have one, ask your successful mentor plenty of questions. Ask over and over again. Yes, there will be those who won't tell you anything, but keep asking until you get to the right person that will answer. Remember, the right mind frame is to never give up.

Find out what successful people read about. Find out what they talk about. A millionaire once told me that rich people are not talking about what happened on the soap opera. They are not loading their minds up with tabloid magazine rumors. They are into organizations and magazines that teach you how to be successful and produce multiple streams of income. In addition, he let me know that, we become what we think and talk about the most. When he told me that, I thought about how the bible even lets us know as a man thinketh, so is he. What we think about is very important to propelling us towards success. If you think you are defeated, then you are. If you think small, you will only reap small. On the other hand, if you think and dream big, you will conquer big things.

Pay close attention to your surroundings each day. There are successful people around you every day. The only problem with finding these unique individuals is they go unnoticed lots of time. One of the reasons is, they do not try to be fl ashy, as most people would think. Remember not to focus on what the media highlights as major success. Find successful people right in your community, workplace, church, family, organizations, and amongst friends. Finding or knowing someone successful to gain knowledge and information is priceless. This would be the perfect person to model yourself after. This is your mentor. It is even better to find someone with similar interest and goals.

When we admire or model after someone, we see the finished product. Know that this individual has strived to get to that point of success. Hard work and sacrifices are always required for achievement. Have you ever applied for a job and thought within, they do not do anything here. Once you get in there, you realize it is a whole different story. When given a chance to do what the others do, you begin to see it is a little harder than you thought. Nothing will come easy. Your mentor guidance will make it seem easy because they know what to avoid and exactly what to do.

Modeling after something or someone is simply providing a helpful pattern to follow. Do not forget to institute some of your originality and personality. If your mentor tells you not to use your originality or personality, do not do it. Remember, they have the expertise and do not want you to get off track. In some instances, your personal touch will be necessary. For instance, if you were a minister and someone patterned themselves after you to the point they tried to sound and dress like you, which would take away from their effectiveness. This actually takes away from the individual that is using the modeling process. When the congregation hears him, they will always refer back to the person they modeled after. Therefore, to achieve your own accolades, it is important not to lose your uniqueness. Think about it like this, if an employer trained each employee on the same duties. After the orientation, your personality and originality should take effect. Of course, you will stay within the pattern, but doing the duties in a way that is most effective for you.

There are so many successful people for you to choose from to model after. The key is to be a good follower of instructions. Think about how a college curriculum is set up for you to copy what the previous student did. Therefore, if you want to be a doctor, you will follow the path other doctors have taken. Of course, updates are made periodically in every field of study, but a road map is put into place to achieve that particular degree of study. If you wanted to be a teacher, you would look at a course manual concerning becoming a teacher. You could even ask a teacher, "What do I have to do to become a teacher?" All student – teachers model what previous teachers have already learned. So if you follow the guide, in the end you should get the same results. No matter what area, if you are modeling someone, you should get the same results if you do everything the same way. On the other hand, if you decide you want to take a nursing class while trying to obtain a teaching degree, this would slow you down or deter you from the goal of becoming a schoolteacher. The main thing is to stay on track and follow the instructions. No matter what your goal is, you can find someone to model after. If you want good credit, ask someone with good credit, "What do I have to do to get good credit." If you want to retire early, find out what it takes. Do not be surprised that you might get doors slammed in your face, but if you want something bad enough, you will keep asking. Sometimes bugging someone is good. You will get the information and the person will be glad to be left alone.

Did you know, if you are not living your dream, you are living and contributing to someone else's dream? There are so many things that we always thought about striking out and doing but never did. Did you know that every invention started out as a simple idea? Just imagine what if you moved forward with your ideas. Think about all of the people that we look up to. A lot of times, we simply just need to ask questions of them for guidance. What does it hurt to ask? Nothing of course! After determining what you want to be successful in, seek out someone that does what you are interested in. Go to the library and read up on your interest. You can go around the world through a book. Surfing the Internet is also a good source for a wealth of information. You will be surprised, concerning who around you that has information on different subject matters. I can go on and on but we must be open minded and exhaust every resource.

Don't be a copycat! I can remember hearing this phrase when I was growing up. When trying to become successful, you should always be a copycat. This is basically what modeling after someone else is. Yes, there will be times you will have to stand on your own two feet and make informed decisions, but in most instances, be a copycat. The quickest way to become successful is to model after someone or something already successful. They have already proven it can be done. By knowing this, I hope that you realize that there is a formula to success. A lot of people think success is just something of chance, but it is a formula. Remember I mentioned if you want to be a schoolteacher, you would simply follow the college curriculum just like the other teachers that came before you. Remember you are trying to get from point A to point B. The same thing applies when it comes to dealing with finances. If you copy what other successful individuals have done, you can achieve their financial status and even more. So think about it like this, you can have comfort in knowing that something works before you even start it. Again, it has already been proven by others. Modeling after someone else will give you the big picture of what you are trying to achieve. Again, you will know what pitfalls to avoid and what works best.

Modeling after someone works, but remember that success is a mind formula. When modeling after someone else, you must realize that you still have to make sacrifices and do all the hard work yourself. Do not get relaxed and think something is going to be easy because you are modeling after someone else. As stated earlier, when we are on the outside looking in, it may appear as if it does not require much to achieve a goal. Think about a standup comedian doing a skit on stage. Sometimes we think within, "They're not that funny." "I could do better than that." This is easy to assume until you look into it and find out the work does not begin when you get on stage. Not only will you find out that you have to tell jokes, you will realize that you must write skits, be a promoter, etc. Once some people know all of this, they would stop. Always remind yourself that success is more than what meets the eye. Always, be attentive to your mentor and willing to work hard because it is your dream. Think of it as a gift that your mentor is helping you. Truly, they did not have to do it. Definitely do not waste anyone time. Always take advantage of every encounter. If you have gained all the knowledge you can from a mentor, advance to a new mentor. Sometimes, the mentor my not have the time to teach you anymore. Do not become stagnated waiting for someone that does not have the time to help you. As you get information, put it to use and press forward.

Put God First In Success

SOME BOOKS AND AUDIO cd's on success will acknowledge God, but rarely express putting God first. This may be challenged by some, but it cannot be disputed if you are trying to obtain true success and happiness. This key or principle is in accordance with the teaching, that if we acknowledge God, He shall direct our path. Having divine direction is priceless! In our journey of life, there will be many obstacles. This is especially true when striving to be successful. I have found out that if we ask to be led in whatever we do, things will go easier. One of the reasons is God knows everything that is going to take place in our life. By having God's guidance, you can avoid some of the many pitfalls in pursuit of success. I have learned to pray and ask God to go before me in my life, in my day, in my week, and make things easy. It is good to ask of him if there is anything you are going to face to protect you and to work it out in your favor. Truly, God knows everything about us and can help guide in all decision making. Even though God is willing to guide us, we must be willing to follow his lead.

"Take the Lord along with you everywhere you go," is an old gospel hymn with a very powerful message. I remember hearing this song while growing up in South Alabama. This song was more than just a hymn; it was wise words to live by. To be successful to your highest potential, you will need God's help. God can open doors and provide opportunities for you that you cannot do on your own. Having divine intervention is priceless. On the other hand, He can close doors or situations that no one can open. He can reach people and situations that you cannot reach in the physical. For example, God can change someone's mind and make your way easy. He can send the right connections or help you on the way.

When you trust God, you will have a feeling that you could do all things through Him because he strengthens you. We should believe this at all times. At times, when you are in doubt of doing something yourself, if you believe that you can do it with Christ's help, you could conquer anything. It does not matter what the situation is. God will honor your faith and belief in Him. If you abide in Him and He abides in you, you can ask whatever you will and it will be granted to you. That may sound simple, but it is true. He will give you the desires of your heart. The key is you must have the desire. If we first seek out the Lord righteousness, all other things shall be added to you. This includes success! Again, seeking direction first is the key.

As strange as it may sound, the first guide on being successful was the teachings from the bible. Many scholars will have you think they invented the wheel on success, but this is not true. This wisdom is in the bible. I am sure you have heard of the secret and all the big theories. Again, success is indeed a formula. The bible lets us know that also. For example, you will pull positive and negative things towards you because the way your mind operates. Remember I stated earlier as a man thinketh, so is he. We must learn how to draw positive things to us. Through God's wisdom, He tells us how. To get to our desired level of success, we know at this point that we need to follow the road map. At this point, we know that putting God first is essential for guidance. This is important because you are trying to go to a level in life you have never been before.

Did you know that there are three dimensions to mankind? We have a physical being, a mental being and a spiritual being. This sounds a little creepy and complicated, but you will understand my theory after deeper thought. You are probably saying what does this have to do with putting God first or success. It has a lot to do with it! As stated earlier, all physical things you see come from our inner being. This is very deep! Did you know that things evolve or surface in the physical must be birthed internally? If you cannot see something in your mind, cannot imagine yourself being it, cannot dream it, etc. before it even develops, then it will not happen. This goes back to the biblical principle that as a man thinketh, so is he. This simply means, if you think you cannot do something, then you cannot. If you think you are a winner, then you are. When trying to become successful, the way you think is critical. Your mind must be transformed. This will take some practice.

We have heard others say they want to "put God first" in everything they do. What does this really mean? Does it mean sell everything and become a missionary? Of course not! It does mean acknowledging all things happen if it is God's will and seek divine direction whenever possible. Knowing this, the things that we desire should be in God's will. When God is really first in our life, we devote time to try to figure out how He wants us to live. What is our destiny? What should we be doing? What is our purpose? If we do the things that are in God's will for us, we will always be highly successful in everything we do.

Ask yourself sincerely if you are doing everything to discern God's will for your life. When we have purpose, we take action. Guess what, you are suppose to be doing more and conquering more. You can decide this day to do more. God's purpose and destiny for our lives, is for us only. You are unique and have a specific purpose. Do not let anything cheat you or stop you from living up to your potential. The greatest success always begins with putting God first. Putting God first includes looking to Him as our ultimate source. When you start out this way and if rough times occur, you will look to the hills of your source of help.

HAVE FAITH TO SUCCEED

F -A - I -T - H, all you need is a little bit of faith! Having faith is powerful! Remember, success is a formula! This formula is activated in the mind. Faith is also developed in our mind. Faith is all about a positive outlook that starts within the mind. You must have faith and believe you can be, have, do, or achieve whatever your heart desires. What is faith? Faith is the substance of things hoped for, the evidence of things not seen. Again, this simply means, you've got to see it before you be it. At this point, you should start noticing a trend. Visualize living your success or goal and it will evolve into the physical. Our belief in a dream or goal that is not in existence can develop by having faith. If you have the faith concerning anything, you can bring anything to the physical. This is the power of attraction.

Some people call it the law of attraction. Some scholars coined it as the secret, but there is no secret. If you have faith and believe, anything becomes possible.

This is very powerful because not having faith can prevent you from becoming successful. I remember this kid name Earnest from the 2ⁿᵈ grade that could run very fast. No matter what, Earnest would always come in first place. One day I gave it all I had and in a very close race, I managed to beat Earnest. I had finally beat Earnest! The other kids were excited and jumped around screaming. I was so excited because Earnest was very fast. This only aggravated Earnest, but I felt very big for the moment. I had a big "Kool Aide" smile. When we went back to class, the kids told the teacher. She was very surprised because she knew Earnest could run very fast! She could not believe it because everyone knew Earnest was really fast. To my surprise, the teacher took the entire class back outside, because she wanted to see this for herself. I had out run Earnest earlier, but now I was getting nervous. The count was on to start the race. On your mark, get ready, get set, and go! My heart beating fast, we both took off running as fast as we could. Earnest won a close race and regained his title. Even though I had beaten Earnest earlier, I began to doubt myself when the teacher said she was taking us back outside. If I would have remained confident and believed I could do it, I would have. This is the same way when trying to obtain success. You must believe all things are possible. If we let doubt magnify in our mind, we will second-guess ourselves. When we second-guess ourselves, our results will reflect that. Again, all things are possible, but you have to believe that. This involves your faith. If you believe it, you can achieve it!

Even if you do not feel like your faith is strong enough, you could look at what someone else has achieved and gain confidence by what they did. We all know someone that has achieved a substantial amount of success unexpectedly to us. By knowing they did it, you should embrace the fact that they are no different from you. This should also give you the assurance that it can be done. It is all about your faith and your mind control. Of course, there will be times you will doubt your knowledge and ability, but always believe that your dream will eventually happen. If you have faith in God, he will strengthen you in whatever areas you are weak in. If there is something that appears to be too much for you, he can put people in your path to do those tasks for you. Remember, you want to always be productive no matter what. Suppress the thoughts and feelings of "I can't do something." Don't allow these thoughts to linger in your mind. Therefore, always think positive things. Whatever we think internally will show up externally.

Faith is an awakening experience of believing in something. Faith gives us the opportunity to experience the true strength that lies within us. For this to occur, we must allow our thoughts and emotions towards a purpose and a creative ending result to orchestrate a feeling of a strong internal will power. This takes place within our mind. Our faith is gained or limited by our own thought processes. Yes, I said your own thought process. Every individual has a certain measure of faith. This simply means, your faith may be different from the next person, but you have some faith. That faith may be a little or it may be a lot. What you want to do is always have more faith than doubt. Also, you should aim to increase your faith, which increases your results. Believe it or not, most people have an above average amount of faith. The problem is they do not maintain that level of faith in every situation. Overall, when it comes to having faith for success, the average falls below 50% range. Actually, this is not too bad because you have room to go up or down. If your faith is in the 0% - 25% ranges you are already doubtful. Highly successful individual's faith level stay high all the time near the 75% -100% range. This individual believes good things are coming their way. They believe that good things suppose to happen for them. They believe they will have favor. This is what you should strive for in every situation no matter what the outlook may be.

Maintaining a strong sense of faith gives you the passion to take action to achieve. Having faith allows you the opportunity to take an active and creative approach in life, whereas most people "tiptoe quietly through life." It amazes me how many people I know personally that are paralyzed by that four-letter word fear. You have probably heard that the letters: f-e-a-r stands for false evidence appearing real. Think about it, you are in fear of something that has not happened or does not exist. Fear is the main reason that many people give up hope or faith. Think on that deeply! Some people at times have given up in life, because of something that has not even happened. This is why I tell people to be a part of your own life instead of being caged by fear. We have all been there before saying, "I want to put a restaurant or store here or there." As soon as someone else does it, we say, "You're not going to believe I started to put a store there." Then here comes the big ole fat buts. "I would have done it but…… I talked to the people but… I'm not smart enough, old enough, well-off enough", and on and on." Excuses are expressions of fear. It is time for you to be challenged again. I remember once in high school I scolded a teacher for not teaching us anything. I wanted to be challenged! This teacher would give us only puzzles and projects surrounding food often. I knew that if I was without a learning opportunity, I could not advance intellectually. Of course, some students agreed with me, but some were content with puzzles. Life is similar to this. You could take the easy way out or you could work hard to advance. Are you going to be content forever in your comfort zone or will you take the challenge. Reading this book alone gives you the opportunity to grow.

Fear causes some people not to take action for the fear they will be ridiculed, laughed at, or embarrassed. Some people even have a fear of being successful due to the responsibilities that they perceive success will bring. Truly, when much is given, much is required. Even though much is required, you can do it if you believe you can. It takes more energy to be fearful as it does to have faith. There is no room for fear when striving to become successful. If you have the mind frame that you are only going to give something a shot, why even get started on it. Regardless of the challenges, you have to face them. Think about it like this, whether you are successful or not, you will still face challenges. Just know it would be better to strive, achieve success, and face challenges instead of failing. Some challenges will be beyond your control regardless, but you should always turn fear into faith.

Always strive to keep your dreams alive by keeping the faith. Having faith is an ingredient of forward thinking. To achieve anything, it will require faith and belief in your vision. This is a requirement. It does not matter if others do not have faith in you. Remember, it is all about your faith. It also takes hard work, determination, and dedication. Remember all things are possible for those who believe.

Prayer And Success

IN ORDER TO TRULY put God first, we should always pray. Prayer is our communication line to God. When striving for success, prayer is simply a humble plea request of action by God. It does not matter what your request might be. This request is simply asking for something or for action pertaining to gaining something. It is specific to the requestor needs or desires. If you desire to be successful, you should pray for your success in every area of your life. If you desire a job, you could pray for one. You could pray for just about any situations or uncertainties in your life. It does not matter how small or great. Basically, you could pray regarding anything.

Our prayer request should always be sacred and sincere. A prayer does not have to be long or contain great impressive words. It should be a sincere appeal that includes thankfulness from the heart. Remember, this is a sacred confidential sincere appeal to God. Praying sincere means, you should pray with seriousness from your heart and with an open mind. Your mind should be clear from distractions to focus on your sincere prayer.

To experience the greatest success and fulfillment, you should be prayerful. This key involves the biblical principle of, ask and you shall receive. You should simply ask. Again, this is talking about making a request known by asking. If you wanted something from someone and you never asked for it, how would they know? We know that God knows what we need before we ask, but asking shows humility. Also, another principle teaches us we have not because we ask not. What are you waiting on to ask? Then the bible teaches us that we ask and receive not because we ask amiss. This means we ask wrongly or for the wrong things. In the book of Matthew 21:22, it teaches us, whatsoever ye shall ask in prayer, believing, ye shall receive. The first step is to ask. God honors the sincerity of the prayer. He already knows our needs before the asking.

In order to pray one needs to know how to pray. You should not start a prayer asking for things. This is selfish! Always start a prayer being thankful and in reverence to God and his son Jesus. When we pray, we should first give thanks. Be thankful for what He has already done in your life. After you give thanks, you should ask your request. Finally, you should show gratitude of praise and vow to give future praise in closure. This is the proper outline of prayer.

A perfect example of this is the Lord's Prayer. Always pray and ask in Jesus' name. Jesus' name is powerful. We must go through the Son to reach the Father. Some people are successful that don't pray or even believe in God. This explains the biblical teaching of God rains on the just and unjust. It's easy to sometime look at others and think why and how they did this or that and lose focus on your desires. Just be happy for others, but focus on your needs and desires. Even though we know some people do not pray, I believe praying brings success with purpose.

When you pray, you must believe what you are praying for can be done. If you do not believe it can be performed, why even pray. Do not give in to the feelings of doubt. God can do anything but fail. It is easy to be doubtful but do not doubt and know that the earth is the Lord and He can do all things. If your prayer is not answered the first time, just continue to pray and expect results. If you really want something, you would ask more than once if you needed to. A prayer request is the same way. It is simply how bad do you want it. I am asking you, "How bad do you want it? " If you have to pray again, pray again.

After you have made your prayer request, you should have an expectancy. You should be looking for the results! This indicates that you believe your prayer request will be answered. I personally, believe whether you pray or not everyone that experiences success has to hope for things to go as they like. This goes back to faith. Faith is hoping and expecting a certain outcome. Therefore, whether you believe in God or not success principles line up with many bible passages. God is always in control. He will guide us on this journey of achieving more if we simply follow.

One might think, why I should pray for something I could do myself. Yes, some things we can and should do for ourselves. Even the things we can do, does not has to go our way. Believe it or not, we cannot do anything ourselves unless God allows us to do it. Knowing this, we only will accomplish those great things that He allows through Him. No matter how smart you think you are, it is He that grants wisdom and understanding. When we understand this, we will remain humble and be prayerful.

It is easy to forget and get caught up with success, thinking you achieved success alone. No one ever achieves success alone. From birth, we start to model others that we see. Therefore, we build and add each day and year. Therefore, others help us and so do divine intervention. Without God's help, success will elude us. Whether you think you are religious or not, God blesses the just and the unjust. So if you see someone wicked that may appear to be highly successful because of merchandise, know that God is just so merciful, He blesses us all. It is all about faith and belief. If someone believes they can be or do something, they can. To have that balance and true success with fulfillment, God has to be part of the equation. Including God in our daily lives will keep us grounded after achieving success and take us to the rim of true success.

THE RIGHT MIND FRAME FOR SUCCESS

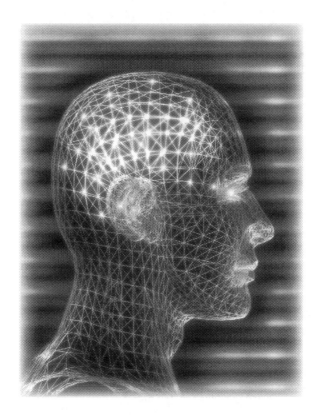

THE MOST IMPORTANT KEY to being successful is having the right mindset. Again, the most important key of them all is the right mindset. This sounds so simple, but without this, you cannot be successful. Again, if you do not get in the right mind frame you will not be successful. Having the right mind frame is most common key that separates successful people from unsuccessful people. Yes, it is the mind frame. Most people would think money is what separates us, but it is the mind frame. Successful people view things differently than others. If you do not develop the right mind frame, you can obtain money, but it will vanish. This is why someone can win the lottery and be broke in a few years. A person's state of mind will determine their success. Even though this may seem simple, getting in the right mind frame is one of the hardest things for some people to do. In this section, you will obtain information to help you develop the right state of mind to become successful at everything you try.

Let's take a closer look at why it is so hard for some people to get in the right mind frame. The answer to this is pretty simple. It is us! We often hinder ourselves due to the way we view things. After all of the excuses we try to think of, the bottom line is success or failure is up to us. It is simply up to you! We often look at the rewards without examining the sacrifices that have to be made. Yes, you should think about the end result, but do not forget about the middle. Visualize the prize or your name in lights, but you must count up the cost of what it will take to get to the prize. You must learn to look at the entire picture. Realize, anything worth having will take hard work and sacrifice to obtain. Tell yourself that you must pay the cost. In other words, making sacrifices just comes with the territory.

Getting in the right mind frame goes deeper than just knowing you have to work hard and make sacrifices. Your old way of thinking must be transformed. Using your old way of thinking, you will get the same old results. It is as if you have been brainwashed for years and you need to forget everything you think you know. Whether we believe it or not, we have been programmed to think a certain way by the media and other sources. Even though we have done things and thought a certain way, we must be willing to give up our old way(s) of thinking. It is time to learn how to control your mind. I hope this does not seem strange, but you must train your mind to think and view things in a certain way; a positive way, an expectancy way, a successful way. In the past, you may have viewed some things as painful to do. You must learn to reprogram your mind and block out the painful feelings to view them as pleasurable ones. Some people will be skeptical of this practice, but many people pay doctors lots of money just to help train their mind about phobias. This is basically the same concept. You see the mind is very powerful. You could train your mind to ignore something, overcome something, etc. Let's say for example getting up in the morning to go to work may seem painful or unpleasurable to some people. Reprogram your mind to view not getting up to go to work will be more painful or unpleasurable when you cannot pay your bill. Changing the mind frame on this one thing gives you a feeling of drive to take action. What if you begin to view all of your challenges this way? There would not be much that could slow you down or stop you.

It is impossible to be successful in anything without being in the right mind frame. It does not matter what type of success you desire. It is imperative that your mind set is correct.

There is a certain way of thinking that you must develop. This type of positive thinking is what will give you the discipline you will need to take action. Being in the right frame of mind and taking action are the two most vital things to becoming successful. Without these two ingredients, you have already failed.

The truth is simple; many people are holding themselves back from achieving because of how they think. People who are able to build wealth and accomplish the goals set, work differently than people who are complacent and find themselves in a rut instead of accelerating toward the life they desire.

Another characteristic of successful people is that they take action in spite of being uncertain. Remember, uncertainty will happen in life regardless, so go ahead a give your all every single time. At some point, we all have dreaded the uncomfortable feeling of breaking out of our normal routine and the uncertainty that comes in different situations. People who remain in a rut, often let fear of change stop them. These are the people you often hear talking about the opportunities they have had, but then make excuses to why they did not capitalize.

Having a Open Mind

The mindset of people who succeed obviously differs from people who do not. Being open-minded is the key. Successful people realize they do not know everything, but they remain open-minded and they are willing do something about it. If you went to the bank and they denied you, does this mean you should give up? An open-minded person would ask, "What will it take for me to get this loan, because I'm going to do that and I will be returning." Thinking this way shows that you are being open-minded, serious, and strong willed. It shows that you are about taking action. In other words, successful individuals entertain the fact that their opinions may be wrong, and they are not too proud to learn new things. Viewing the world with this kind of open mind is important. We should always be willing to learn and improve.

Having the Right Mindset Takes Practice

Reprogramming your mind does not come overnight. You have to make a conscious effort to change the way you think. When something negative occurs, you should not allow that thought to remain in mind. In addition, you have to block the urge to complain. The more you complain about it, the negative thought will last twice as long. Once you are finished complaining, it will still remain stuck in our head. Tell yourself that even though you cannot control the negative event or thought, you can control your reaction to it and what happens in the future. Give yourself a pep talk if you need to. Change the subject or think of something positive.

Believing yourself

Not believing in yourself is like going to box Mike Tyson and then punching yourself in the head. People can perceive doubt in our body language and communication. If you do not believe in what you are doing, chances are others will not believe in you either.

Be a Problem Solver "Think Resolution"

Put on your thinking caps. When you have a problem or obstacle, do not think about the problem itself, but how you can resolve it. Consider how you could benefit from its resolution.

From this day forward, view a problem as an opportunity. The ability to view a problem as an opportunity is one of the best skills you can have. The right mindset is simply having a creative mindset recognizing opportunities for growth. Always think outside the box for solutions and resolutions.

Creative thinking is key

One quote from Albert Einstein explains it very well: "We can't solve problems by using the same kind of thinking we used when we created them." This lets us know we need to be opened and creative.

Do not become preoccupied with the past

Instead of living for today, some people let the past bog them down. Some people spend a lot of time thinking about past events and situations that they can't do anything about. The past is simply that, the past. It is already gone. There is no point in thinking about things that happened months ago. Of course, we should learn from past experiences, but we should always be forward thinking. So live in the present and think about the future. Our past does shape us, but our today and tomorrow provides a new opportunity.

Today is going to be a good day. Today is going to be a bad day. Which do you prefer? Of course the good day, but if we think things will be badly, they will. We have heard that life and death is in the power of the tongue. This simply means you can speak something into existence. Your outlook should always be positive. When you are going through different situations, tell yourself, "this is only a test." Say to yourself, you are making sacrifices that will pay off eventually. Be sure not to associate work or a sacrifice as a negative. Remember, your mind has got to be transformed. Remind yourself that if you do not work or make the sacrifices things will really be bad on you. We must learn to view everything in this manner. Think about it, if you viewed things in a positive way, this gives you motivation. When we are motivated, we take action. When we take action, we get results. When we receive positive outcomes, we desire more positive outcomes.

Even something such as work can become enjoyable. This is possible when you begin to always learn to look on the bright side. Some people focus more on negatives and come up with many reasons why something cannot be done. When we focus in on the negative, things will seem worse than what they really are. Always focus on the positives no matter what. Of course, there is risk to everything, but you must focus on the outcome you are trying to achieve. The good should always outweigh the bad.

You are a winner and you are going to win. This is the positive frame of mind you should always have. There is no reason to let your thoughts move to the negative side. Know that with anything, the negative or hard times are only temporary. Tell yourself you are going to win in the end. It is good to imagine yourself at the level you are trying to achieve. Of course, negativity exists seemingly everywhere we look today. Again, we must keep our focus on our goals. Even though negativity exists, we get to choose what we want to focus on, the people we associate with, and sometimes even our environment. Knowing this, it is best to avoid negativity in these areas. Have you ever noticed when you talk to someone grouchy that you walk away from the conversation feeling somewhat down? This is because the use of negative influence can change your outlook. On the other hand, positive uplifting conversations leave us feeling inspired.

When negativity presents itself, try not to focus on it too long. Shake it off. Remember we get to choose what we allow our mind to entertain. The longer we allow our mind to stay in a negative state when trying to achieve something; we minimize our chances for success. You must learn to have hope. Having hope or faith is a property of having a positive outlook. You may not know how or when you are going to do something, but having hope is enough to keep you driven. If we focus on everything or every reason why we should not succeed then things will look cloudy. For example, someone may live in a ghetto, but by not focusing on their immediate situation, they can overcome their obstacles. Only focus on getting to Point B. I have learned if you resist negative thoughts, you will feel empowered to accomplish any task. Remember you are a winner, but you must think you are a winner to really be one. We become what think about! This statement is very true even when it concerns thinking positively or negatively. When trying to become successful, some people start off with a negative attitude. If we thought from the start something is not going to work, there is a strong chance it will not. This type of attitude comes out in our body language and even verbally. If we think we are going to have a bad day at work, most likely we will because we already expect to. By thinking this, you will help fulfill this self-fulfilled prophecy by your own thoughts and actions. By your own actions, you will look for something to go wrong because you have already told yourself it was going to be a bad day. As soon as the slightest thing occurs, you will confirm to yourself, I knew it was going to be a bad day. Think about the times we say, I do not want to get up, then by our actions, we will drag. Our way of thinking is powerful. The way we think determines every aspect of our lives. If we choose to take in the negative thoughts, things in our life will always seem harder.

When we focus more on positive things, our thinking opens up in ways you never would have imagined. It is important to practice avoiding negative thoughts and look on the bright side. When in doubt, hopelessness, or any negativity enters your mind, you must learn to change that thought immediately to a positive or simply resist it. Just like when you flip through channels on television, if you do not like what is on, turn the channel. We have to change channels or thoughts in our minds.

Decrease your interaction with negative people and negative environments. This will give you a new look on things and individuals. As you practice, this you will begin to come from under the fog of negativity. Some people close to you may even start to appear negative. Just know even though some relationships you cannot dissolve entirely, you must learn to limit your time and know when to move on to avoid negativity. You will notice that you will be sharper in many areas of your life. This will help you physically, mentally, spiritually, socially, and even financially.

Thinking positive, not only makes things look brighter, but it also helps to increase your faith. This will help you to believe in yourself and your abilities to reach your goals. We have so many gifts and talents. Thinking positive also gives you the faith and courage to try to pursue some of those things. Also, this gives you the courage to do your best and go past your previous limits or expectations. Doors will start opening for you because you will expect good things to happen.

As stated earlier, to be successful or financially free, you need to find out what successful people are doing, reading, and talking about. Again, if you hang around negative people all the time, their ways will eventually influence your actions. You must be very selective of the people you keep in your company. For example, if you hang around drunks all the time most likely their conversation is going to evolve around behaviors associated with drinking. If you hang around people that talk about others in a negative manner, most likely their conversation is going to be belittling of others. The point is, you should not be around negative if you can help it. A negative environment can eventually influence you. Have you ever gone to work and someone has a negative attitude and due to their attitude or behavior causes you to have a negative attitude. You can come to work happy and then all of a sudden they get you frustrated and they steal your happiness away. Therefore, it is very important to be particular of the people we interact with. It is very important to decipher what we allow our mind to focus on. Those things or people that are not positive in our lives, we should shake it off and keep going. The ones closest to us can sometimes be a hinder to us when trying to achieve success. Oftentimes, the negativity comes from loved ones, so be prepared for this. You may hear things like, you cannot do it. You are thinking too big. You are not rich, etc. Just tell yourself these are your dreams and your goals. They may not want to go where you are trying to go in life. So when it comes from the loved ones, just know that they have not adopted the mind frame of thinking out of the box. This is a perfect opportunity for you to enlighten them on your knowledge. It is up to them to believe that not only you can make it, but they could too. You can do anything you put your mind to. That is why getting in the right mind frame is so important. Being positive no matter what will move a lot of obstacles out of the way.

There is an old quote that says, "Birds of a feather flock together". This simply means the people we hang with influence us just as our environment does. Naturally, people who do bad things like to be around others who do bad things. At some point, you must break away from negative vibes and negative influences to develop a positive outlook. Listed below are some examples of things to promote a positive vibe.

Ways to promote being Positive

1. Just smile! One way to attract positive people or get positive feedback is to simply smile. Smiling requires far less energy than frowning. A smile on one's face usually indicates happiness. By simply smiling at someone could uplift that person day.

2. Always think positive. In order to do this, it requires that you believe good things can and will happen for you and for those around you. Your mind is considered the storehouse of power. It is up to us to decide whether negative or positive energy will control our minds. Let's allow our positive energy to control every single day. Positive thinking brings inner peace, success, improved relationships,

better health, happiness, and fulfillment. It also helps the daily affairs of life move more smoothly, and make life look promising.

Positive thinking is contagious. People around you will pick up your mental moods and are affected accordingly. It will be up to them to adopt the positive outlook permanently. When was the last time you simply sat down and thought about happiness, good health, and success? Do you view these things in a positive manner or a negative manner? The way we think determines what kind of results we get.

Effective positive thinking is much more than just repeating a few positive words, or telling yourself that everything is going to work out. It needs to be your predominant mental attitude at all times. It is not enough to think positively for a few moments, and then let fears creep back into our minds. This takes constant work because doubt is always near. Ask yourself, are you willing to make some real internal changes? Are you willing to change from your old ways of thinking? If you are, here are some others tips to help you develop the power of positive thinking:

*Always use only good words while thinking and while talking. Use words such as, 'I can, 'I am able', 'it is possible', it can be done', etc.

*Only promote feelings of happiness, strength, and success.

*Always ignore negative thoughts. Always change the channel in your mind.

*Always form a plan of action.

*Read inspiring quotes and biblical passages.

*Minimize the time you listen to the negative news and newspapers.

*Associate with people who are uplifting.

*Always sit and walk with your back straight. This will give you confidence and inner strength.

*Always think positive and expect only favorable results, even if your current circumstances are not favorable. Your mental attitude affects your life therefore changing circumstances.

3. Speak pleasant things every time you speak. If we speak good things, we will have an expectancy to receive good. Speaking negative and hurtful things diminish our outlook. This is why it is important to be selective concerning whom you associate with. For example, you may say, "Good morning", and a negative person response may be, "What's so good about it?" On the other hand, a positive person will receive that positive gesture and in return, give a positive gesture. Even the most positive people can be drained by negative speech of others. Knowing this, by all means avoid these negative encounters. Speaking positive to others is good, but you should try to speak positive things to yourself too. Practice doing this exercise daily until you believe it. Write down motivational or inspirational words and say it aloud. For example, I am happy, or I am healed. You can use whatever word (s) you desire. This is very powerful.

Conquering Fear

FEAR IS A VERY complex subject because there are so many reasons why people may experience fear. The fear that I will focus on, is the fear that causes many not to take action. Often times, it is because of the fear of change. We may have fear of losing a job, getting behind on bills, developing a health problem, etc. These fears of change are very common. In this chapter, you will learn how to think differently and manage your fears.

Fears are always person specific. This simply means you may fear something that someone else does not have a problem with. On the other hand, you may feel like something is small that another person fears. No matter what it is, you can overcome all of your fears and become successful in whatever you desire. Again, it is simply us that hinder success by giving into our fears. It could be fears known or just in our subconscious mind. The fear of the unknown is the type of fear that promotes procrastination. Many dreams never develop due to this type of fear. The fear of the unknown could also be called the "what if" fear syndrome. Many people have talents and ideas, but never act on them because of the "what if" syndrome. Have you heard this one before, "What is everybody else going to think or say if I fail?" How about, "I'm not smart enough."

The majority of the time fear is not good. Believe it or not, there are some instances fear can be beneficial if you view it in the right manner. Fear is an underlying motivator that causes lots of actions and non-actions every day. Remember we discussed earlier how to program our minds to view unpleasurable or fearful things differently. Instead of having the feeling of fearing being laid off my job, let this fear drive you to work harder to be a vital part of your company. Have the mind frame; I will work harder so if they lay off, I will be looked upon as a good worker.

Doing something different or new can seem a little scary. Think about it this way, we all feel comfortable with things we are familiar. Something like learning to speak another language could seem very challenging and fearful. Learning about purchasing stocks could seem way over our head. Knowing this, following your dream or trying to achieve at a higher level can seem unreachable. Don't let this feeling cause you not to even try. Reprogram your mind to deal with your fears and obstacles to become successful.

Did you know you are actually programmed to fear certain things? We form opinions from our up bringing, experiences, media outlets, and many other sources. Even though we are presented so many things to fear, fear itself remains something perceived. We know at this point that fear is something only perceived in your mind. Again, think about that, the unknown is just that, something not known. This means it simply does not exist! If something does not exist, why would you let it control you? We must reprogram our minds on how we view things.

Should we live in so much fear? Of course not! This is why it is important to put God first and the trust in him. Again, fear is only a state of mind. If we remain bound by fear, we will be scared to try to accomplish our goals. Some people do not even consider trying at all because of fear. I have known some people who would not apply for a certain job because they heard you had to take a test. They feared they would fail the test before even seeing it. There are some people who do not go to college because they wonder, "what if I fail?" The "what if" syndrome over powers their will to even try. One of the hardest things to get out of someone's mind is that they are going to fail. You cannot fail! Failing is not in the success equation. Always remind yourself that failing is not an option. Did you know that you only fail when you quit. Knowing this, you have control over whether you fail or not. Just think about it for a minute. You actually have to quit first to accept failure. For example, think if you were running a race and you felt very tired. The thought of quitting the race will soon come to mind. As you continue, ask yourself within whether or not you should stop or continue. At some point, you must recognize it is up to you. The point is this, to fail you have to quit in your mind first. You have to give in to quitting before you actually stop or fail. Just imagine if you had a no failure attitude? What if you decided no matter what it takes, you are not going to quit? If they say, "Do something else", have the attitude, I am going to do that also. You see, when you are already expecting the worse, you are not going to give it your all. When you go into something doubting, you start telling yourself it is not going to work. When you doubt, you do not produce or perform at the level you are capable. If you continued to tell yourself things are too hard, you cannot do it, you are not smart enough, etc, you would be defeated in everything. Of course, you are not going to do it because you spoke it out of your mouth. It is better to say, "I'll do whatever it takes; I'm going to do it." When you get this attitude of refusing to accept no, things are going to start happening in your favor.

It is so important to get the right mind frame. There are many scenarios that exist that could promote fear. Fear is programmed in our mind. Fear carries a lot of weight on us because it promotes doubt, mediocrity, and ignorance. To be successful, this cycle must be broken. It has to be broken. Some people do not get past this stage. This is one of the most important steps to being successful. The reason why some people never get past this stage is because they have been taught fear for years. The media teaches us fear. People we interact with on a daily basis talk fear into us. You must realize, they may not know anyone thinking outside the box, so they think it is impossible to accomplish things. A person can only teach you to their capacity. Therefore, it is important to be opened minded to new ideas and not let fear control you actions or interactions.

Fear of the unknown is one type of fear that hinders success. Everybody likes to do things they know well so we cannot make our weaknesses known to others. You must realize, the only way to conquer weaknesses and fears is to acknowledge them and face them head on. The bible teaches us that we are more than conquerors. If we only dabble at things we have known for time after time and never take on a challenge, we can expect the same results each time. In today's society, some of our very fears are coming to light. Our job markets are very poor. Companies we have trusted have packed up and moved away. Is there any safe haven? I learned early on not to be dependent solely on any employer and to live within my means.

Remember, try to use fear in a positive way to take action. I fear being poor and homeless so I try to save and manage my finances properly. You may fear taking an exam, so this should make you study twice as hard. Using fear in a positive way should make you take action, be persistent, and do whatever it takes to make it. Having a fear of failure should drive you to work harder, not make you not try at all. This is where being prepared comes in to play. We must make preparations and always plan ahead. Doing this will help minimize your fear. This goes back to counting up the cost. Tell yourself that there is nothing new under the sun. Some people have fear of what others might say.

Procrastination

Hello, meet Mr. Lazy or Mrs. Lazy. We have all met them before. They work at your job, they live in your community, and some do not work at all. Do not get me wrong, I am not talking about someone physically and mentally disabled. You know the one that always takes breaks all day at work. Instead of taking a 30-minute break, how about take 30 minutes of work. I am talking about the one that is sharp as a nail, but asking for your money on payday. You know the one that has an excuse for the excuse. You get my point. We all have seen laziness at all levels. Laziness really decreases your chance at success. I knew a woman that got her son an application for a good job. I asked him did he turn it in before the deadline. He told me his mom did not fill it out. This does not even deserve to be called lazy. This should be called crazy.

One trait of the most successful people is their work habits. This is something you cannot get around. Go ahead and decide right now, do you really want to succeed? If you cannot accept this, you might as well go ahead and close this book. There are no exceptions to this. There is no way around it. It does not matter what you are trying to do or become. To get the big bucks you have to work hard. Most unsuccessful people are unsuccessful due to simply being lazy. Everybody wants the next person to do it. Many want someone else to do all the dirty work. Most people spend more time talking about doing than actually doing it. It would be nice if you could just kick back, do nothing, and collect money. What if our job was like that? What if everybody was lazy at Wal-Mart and didn't put the food out? There are many whom are gifted that are just sleeping on talents and knowledge. Some just too lazy to get up and too lazy to even put forth the effort. They are too lazy to even take time to try. Now that is lazy! I've known people like this that spend more time working at trying to come up with excuses to get out of doing things. Do you know anybody like this? Of course you do! They will come up with every excuse or go through all kinds of changes to avoid work. At some point, you will work with someone like this. They will go through extreme measures to avoid doing a simple task. I have known people to take up to ten minutes in order to hide or hide something to get out of 5 minutes of work. They work hard to get out of doing work, but when it is time to go, you had better watch out. On payday, you cannot beat them to payroll. Many times, people like this view the process of doing the tasks as being more painful than not doing it.

Is it possible to be highly successful and be lazy when trying to achieve it? Think about this for a minute. Now go back in time to high school, could you have worked a little harder? You see past has created our present. So if we are lazy, what type of success will we be building for the future?

Look at highly successful people such as professionals, executives, entertainers, and athletes. Think about all the hard work and preparation. They have some of the finest homes and cars. Some even go on exotic vacations. Surely they just have a lot of play time right? Wrong! It takes hard work. Yes, the rewards are great, but it takes hard work. Sometimes we look at people and wish we were in their shoes. Be careful what you wish for. Some things look glamorous or easy to do, but they are not at all. A professional athlete is a good example. Many young men wish they could become a professional basketball player, but if you knew all the things these guys have to do to compete at that level, you would realize it is not easy. It takes continually hard work every day. Would you be willing to run 5 and 10 miles a day to become a professional basketball player? Are you willing to shoot 1000 jump shots each day?

Sometimes we look at singers and actors and think it is nothing to it. Yes, they may have a nice home, but they are not there to enjoy it. Their maid and lawn crew enjoy their swimming pool and spa more than they do. Some entertainers travel and perform 40 weeks plus out of the year. Could you imagine being on the road 45 weeks each year for 5 years? Imagine not seeing your loved ones but only a few hours at a time in foreign places that you guys meet up at. Did you know models picture sessions could last 6 hours? It is not just taking a few pictures and heading home. Did you know that swimsuit models that appear in catalogs do their beach sessions during the winter? They have to get in the freezing cold water and take pictures so they will be ready for print in the spring. Did you know some actors work 18-hour days at times, repeating the same lines over and over again? In between all of this, they live out of hotel rooms coast to coast to meet engagements. My point is nothing comes easy. Nothing! Anything worth having requires some form of sacrifice whether small or large. A lot of times, we are on the outside looking in and we do not see all the hard work or the sacrifices. Hard work is always going to be essential to being successful. This is only saying you have to do things you never done before and go that extra mile to be the best. You might as well forget about luck or waiting for someone to do something for you if you want to be successful. Even if you won the lottery, it was just meant for you. Do not sit back and wait for something to happen for you or count on luck. Being lazy is not acceptable. Be a part of your life and take action. You must take an active approach. That is the attitude of the most successful athletes and most successful people. No matter if you go to college or not, you cannot be lazy and be successful. A person with a college degree must still go to work after they get out with their degree. Believe me, there are people with degrees that sit at home each day doing nothing. So know that whatever you do, you will not make it if you are lazy. You must take an active approach in order to be successful. If you are the type to sit back and wait for others to take action for you, you are not going to reach your highest potential. Success does not happen by luck, it simply takes hard work. I remember a Mother at church told me something wise when I was graduating from high school. She said if you play first, you would pay for it later, but if you pay first, you could play all you wanted later. In other words, work hard first and things will be easier down the road.

There is nothing that substitutes hard work out of the success equation. You must accept this and face the fact that there are no short cuts. There are no easy ways. My father told me many years ago, "For anything worth having, you have to go through something." Keep in your mind that you must take action and work hard. Procrastination hinders millions of ideas each day. You must realize that some opportunities only come once. Also, remember that time is something no one can get back so use it wisely. Do not wait until the opportunity does not exist anymore. At that point, it is too late. The things we can control, we should try to control, and this is something we can control. Your success depends on you and no one else. Always taking an active approach will always keep you striving towards all your goals. Many people talk about doing things, but ask yourself this, what have I done today to reach my goal? What have you done this week? What have you done this year to get closer to your dreams? Of course, we will not reach our goals if we never get active and stop talking about it. We must stop looking at what others have done to help get us there, but what have we done for ourselves. When we seriously look at our goals, are focused, and take an active approach, we make progress. Are you starting to see how we become what we focus on? We become what we talk about, read about, what we think about, and act on.

Stop Procrastinating

Recognize that procrastination stems from poor habits. You will need to develop new tasks and commit to them. Procrastination as an intentional postponement of an important task that should be in a timely manner. Once you understand the cause of your procrastination, then you can develop strategies to fix it. Recognize the difference between delays in something versus an irrational postponement without justification.

Successful People Are Action People

After you have planned, trained, prepared, and visualized; the time comes that you must take action. Isn't this what you planned for? So once your plan is in place, just take action. Taking action is the physical manifestation of those plans. Failure to act on something after a plan is in place will simply be mere wishes. Just for the record, no successful person has ever not taken action. Successful people are known as Action People. If you go around, you see businesses, jobs, shops, buildings, etc these are simply results of someone who had a plan and decided to take action.

If you take action, you reduce your chances of failure. If you miss the mark, keep taking action moving forward. If you do this, you will eventually find a way to succeed in the end. The best way you can get rid of fear, is by taking action. Taking action opens up many possibilities towards success. It builds experience through any mistakes you make along the way. Any mistakes can then be used as a teaching tool for you to succeed. Henry Ford once said, "Failure is only the opportunity to begin again, only this time more wisely."

Think about a tiny ant. Even though it is so small, it appears to take action without thought when their mound is trampled. I do not know ant language, but none of the ants stop to argue, they just take action. Imagine if we took action like the ant. What if we did it every day? Think about how much you could achieve.

From this day forward, stop postponing future deadlines and goals. Do not make any more excuses why today is not a good day to start. No day is less important than the next today for taking action. Every day is a miracle and an opportunity for greatness. Seize every moment you have been granted. Remember, no action equals no results. No results, equals no success.

EVALUATE STRENGTHS AND WEAKNESSES

WE HAVE HEARD THAT nobody is perfect. Guess what, no matter how bright you are, you have some room for improvements. It does not matter who it is, everybody has some weaknesses. This includes successful people too. Did you know that Henry Ford was uneducated? Did you know Bill Gates was a college drop out? The actor turned governor Arnold Schwarzenegger spoke but a few words of English prior coming to this country. Helen Keller was unable to see, hear or speak at all. President Abraham Lincoln had a mental illness. I can go on and on. Each of these successful individuals had to face their weaknesses in order to achieve a great level of success they did. Think about weaknesses this way; to have a weakness is to be human; to face those weaknesses is to be human; to face those weaknesses is to be successful.

Everybody has strengths and weaknesses. Even after becoming successful, you will still have strong points and weak points about yourself. The question is do you know what your strengths are? On the other hand, do you know your weaknesses? What do others think your strengths and weaknesses are? Be honest now. In this section, you have to be truly honest with yourself to get the maximum results. In our heart, we really know what we are good at. Sometimes people lie to themselves concerning this. We also know where we are lacking certain skills and ability. I remember in high school being good in English, but struggled at times in Mathematics. I would go to my other siblings for clarity. This was something I knew that I had some difficulty in at times. By facing, it I could seek out help.

It is good to know your capabilities, so you will know what areas to seek help. This way you will not have to go at things alone. Sometimes it can be hard to give a true measure of ourselves. The reason is denial. Admitting you have a weakness is to say you're different than what is thought to be the norm., I mean who wants to admit they have a weakness in a certain area. Everybody has weaknesses just like we all have strengths.

What are your weaknesses? What are your strengths? To answer these questions, you must be brutally honest with yourself. Everybody has something they are good at. There are some things you can do that others cannot do that makes you unique. Everybody has strengths and weaknesses. It does not matter how smart you are, you still have some type of weaknesses. Even after you become successful, you will still have some weaknesses. Again, we all have our strong points.

Let's look at strengths. It is important to know your strengths and capabilities. This will allow you to focus on what you are best at. Strengths are things that come easy to you whether they are small or great. A good way to find out your strengths is to evaluate yourself. Another way is to get someone that knows you well evaluate you. It is good to use your strengths as much as possible. This will give you an advantage in situations. An example would be, if you are a great speaker, seize the moment when you interview for the job you wanted. There are many of ways you can think of how should capitalize by using your strength and avoiding be exposed by your weaknesses. A strength could even be having the courage to identify your weaknesses. Do not think acknowledging your weaknesses are a bad thing because it is not. It actually is a character builder. When you acknowledge something, you are not in denial about it and start to grow or heal. Many people have a weakness, but never acknowledge it and seek out help.

Once you have established your weaknesses, you must do something about them. Networking can help strengthen you in these areas. Whatever area you may be weak in, someone is strong. The bible says we are helpers to one another. Others can help you in the areas you are weak. Do not be embarrassed by this because they have weaknesses too and you know something that they do not.

Do you know your strengths and weaknesses? What do people say you are good at? What are the things you are passionate about (strengths)? Think about things that make you second-guess yourself (weaknesses). In our heart, we know these answers. Remember, I knew I needed assistance in math. My goal was to simply get through the subject. This was something I knew I had difficulty with at times so I sought out help to improve in this area. Did I become a math teacher? No, but I faced my weaknesses. To become successful, you must learn to face your weaknesses head on. Even though you may have a knowledge deficit in an area, you must still move forward and conquer the obstacle. The main thing is, you must do whatever it takes to meet your goals.

For years, I have always been a little technologically ignorant. This was something I felt like I was weak in. I remember the first year fax machines came out. I was a vender at a local flea market. I would order my products from various sources. Back in the paper society, companies would send you catalogs through the mail. When the fax machine came out, some companies immediately embraced it to compete with the speed of business. I spoke with a company concerning receiving a catalog. He asked me what my fax number was. I told him I did not have one. He told me that I was not in business. I thought about it, and knew I had to get with the program if I wanted to compete in business. My point is that we must learn to face our weaknesses to become highly successful.

One good thing today is that if you have weaknesses, you can use someone else who has strengths in that area. This is sort of like having a trainer to strengthen you in whatever area you are weak. Today, this can be so powerful due to the unlimited amount of information that is available. Also, if you create a strong network, you will have access to anything or any information. For example, if you have a legal question, you may not be a lawyer, but you gain a lawyer's knowledge when you consult him. It could be something small or something great, but there is no reason to allow a weakness or an obstacle to stop you from becoming successful.

The key to facing weaknesses is to first identify them. If you are unaware or just ignore them, you are limiting yourself. Think about this. Others may try to expose and profit from your weaknesses if you do not improve them. Facing your weaknesses does not necessarily mean conquering them. If your weakness is the fear of flying, then you can conquer the fear, get someone else to fly for you, eliminate the need for flying, or just take alternate transportation. Focus on your strengths: John F. Kennedy was the youngest man to be elected president of the United States. In politics, youthfulness is associated with lack of experience and sometimes the lack of wisdom. JFK opponents targeted this weakness, but President Kennedy won people over with his inspiration and compassion. He was strong in many other areas and it showed.

Involve other people to compensate for your weaknesses: Helen Keller became one of history's most inspirational people with the help her teacher Anne Sullivan, who acted as her eyes and ears. This example shows that there is no excuse not to succeed. Helen could not see, but that did not stop her from achieving greatness through the help of her teacher.

Simply eliminate your weaknesses! Think about it, jobs do this every single day. Think about your favorite sport team, that evaluates each position for weaknesses. As a college student, Bill Gates was not a dummy by a long shot. Even though he desired a college education, his heart was more in to his dream of working with computers. I am quite sure if Mr. Gates had applied himself and forgotten about tinkering with those computers, he could have done very well and impressed his friends and family with that Harvard degree. However, he decided not to follow studies that did not interest him, but chose to change the world instead with computers.

Overcome your weaknesses. Abraham Lincoln overcame failure by being persistent. After losing several elections for various offices and battling depression, he became the president of the United States. We have all heard that practice makes perfect. The more you do something, you will become better and better at it. It is important not to give up when trying to overcome a weakness. No matter how many times it takes, keep working towards conquering the weakness. Tell yourself, if others have conquered it, so can you.

We all have weaknesses that may be affecting our success in our personal and/or business lives. Remember, it is important to be aware of these weaknesses, then choose how to deal with them. Once this can be accomplished, your weaknesses will no longer be an obstacle on your road to success.

At this point, you know you should work on your weaknesses, but you should also improve your strengths. Which do you think is most important to work on? Should you work on improving our strengths or should you work on weaknesses? It is a question with good argument, but the best answer is to work on both, but focus more on your strengths.

Now that you know, you can now go out and be the best you that you can be. As much as we want to improve our weaknesses to avoid failure and loss, it is really our strengths that help us win. Being well rounded might be a good quality, but in a competitive situation, the winner is defined by whoever can best achieve a specific goal.

Although my suggestion is to focus on strengths, we may not always have the option to ignore weaknesses. For example, if you are taking a driving exam, you may be an excellent driver while the car is going forward, but if you do not know how to handle the car in reverse, you will fail the driving exam.

While your priority should still be on your strengths, here are some strategies to address your weaknesses:

1. Educate yourself and Get training: Identify the weakness and take training in that area.

2. Read! Read! Read! Information is everywhere, read about it.

3. Delegate it to another person: Collaborate with a partner who can work on this weak area for you.

4. Network: Gain expertise by utilizing others.

Always Be Open Minded

An associate of mine started an online business many years ago. He told me the concept and I immediately knew a way he could make his company better. He was selling memberships for people to list businesses on his site. I told him, "this might sound crazy, but how about giving the membership away free." List anybody and everybody for free. I thought he should list them and possibly send them a gift or profile of the site. I could tell he thought I had lost it. After explaining that he needed a certain amount of memberships to make a certain amount of money. I told him not to worry about the money; it will come once you create enough traffic. I told him to focus on making money by selling only advertisement to big corporations once you have built the traffic. Unfortunately, he never listened and the company has less than a thousand businesses listed. Many individual, have realized sometimes you have to give something to receive something. There have been numerous online companies that have made fortunes by giving memberships for free. You cannot have a one-track mind. Also, you must realize that business modules must always be reviewed to be revised. Everything is in God's control.

To have an open mind means to be willing to consider or receive new and different ideas. It means being flexible and adaptive to new experiences and ideas. Now more than ever we live in a world that is constantly changing. In order to keep up, we must be open to new experiences and new ways of looking at things. If we do not stay current, we will miss out on the wonderful new opportunities.

Being open-minded is the ability to view a situation with a clear unbiased approach. It is also a way of viewing the world and the people through a perspective unobstructed by judgment, prejudice, and preconceived notions. This can aid you in avoiding conflict, but it is not a trait, which comes naturally. Enclosed, you will find methods of being open to others opinion, leading to a more opened mind and increased contentment with your own life.

Some reasons why you should be open-minded.

A. To validate opinions and views other than your owns by accepting that disagreement does not mean one party has to be wrong. Get rid of the notions that everyone who feel differently about an issue than you is wrong, will open your mind up to deeper thought, even if your own viewpoint never changes.

B. To avoid anger, accusations, and belittlement from heated discussions with others. The easiest way to be close-minded is to disrespect other people views or opinions. At the end of the day if you do not agree with someone, at least you did not become closed-minded and unfair. If you close up, you cannot give or receive a viewpoint. Realize that being open-minded will allow you to express your viewpoint with more persuasion.

C. To be able to look things up and ask questions about alternate viewpoints. Just simply having the mindset to research information is being open-minded and enlarges your knowledge base.

D. To remain open to discussions and questions from those who do not agree with you on a given subject.

E. To be able to step out of your comfort zone. Try something different you have never tried before. Go to a conference. Purchase audio books about what you are trying to achieve. Whether you love or hate a new activity, your opinion will now be based on personal experience rather than closed-minded speculation.

THINK OUTSIDE THE BOX

To be successful you must learn to think outside the box. Thinking outside the box means, thinking in a way you take away all the limits. Tear down all walls of limitation. Take the limits off of God. Take the limits off yourself. It is time to step out beyond. Too often, we set limits on ourselves. We tell ourselves we cannot do this or that before we even try. This is closed-minded thinking. We often think closed-mindedly. When we are closed-minded, we cannot see the big picture. Thinking outside of the box is thinking open-mindedly. There is a whole world out there. The opportunities are unlimited. Success is even easier to obtain due to the easy access of information in today's world.

Literally, just think about a box for one minute. Think on a shoebox to be exact. Let's say a bug is in this shoebox. Okay, this bug is retained and can never leave out of the box due to the walls and the top lid. Do you think the bug has more opportunities to find food inside the box or outside the box? Inside the box, the limits are already set. Think about this in the way we think. Think about this in the way we go after things in life. What if we kept our thoughts, our faith, and our dreams in a box? As long as we keep our dreams in a box, you have to dream small. You will therefore aim for small things because you have preset limits for yourself. There is no reason for us to set limits. Especially when we know what is impossible with man is possible with God. Let's take down the walls. To be successful you must take the limits off. There are no limits. So do not put God in a box by putting limits on Him. God is a big God, so let's not make Him seem small. He created heaven and the earth, so imagine all that He can do. The bible teaches us He can do more than we can ask or think. We cannot even ask or think of enough. Since we now know there is no limit we should always think outside the box. Faith plays a big part in thinking outside the box. Some people talk about faith, but the key is to utilize faith. We must believe that God is in control and over everything. Knowing this, we should put our trust in Him and expect great things of Him. Totally depending on God as your main supplier is one of the hardest things for people to do. We sometimes put our trust in man because to the eyes it seems like a comfort zone. For years, we have been taught to seek a comfort zone and stay in it out of fear. We have been taught to work with our hands and not our mind. We are taught to seek low-level positions and to always work for others until we are old, then retire and die. There is a sense of false comfort. Many people are learning there is no comfort in totally depending on today's companies. Think about the box again. That is a comfort zone. You already know what the limits are. The limits are already preset. When we step outside the box, we step out of a comfort zone. Do not let this scare you. What if you want to retire at 50 instead of 70? Knowing that many companies are unreliable, many people have been broken of the fear to take a more active approach on solidifying their success and future.

With man, we earn wages on the concept doing a task for compensation. With God, we gain according to His riches and glory according to our obedience and faith. Actually, if you are not depending on God as your main supplier, you are taking greater risks. Thinking outside the box is to have faith that all things are possible when you are open to apply new ideas and views. This includes stepping out of your comfort zone even when no one believes in what you are trying to do. Sometimes we trust in others or our job more than God. We must strive to remain open minded. No matter what type of work you do, it is important to trust God over your employer and all of your financial avenues. All financial avenues and even jobs can be terminated. Even though you might work for someone else, pray that God blesses and stretches your finances. This is important because you can make a lot of money, but if God allows car trouble, sickness, etc, to occur you are not getting ahead.

THINK LIKE A WINNER

You must learn to think and act like a winner. Even when you are not there yet, you must learn to fake it until you make it. Guess what, nobody knows whether you are a winner or not. Every day, put on your winner face and winner attitude. Thinking like a winner means seeing yourself as a winner even before you are a winner. When you believe it, others will believe it. Thinking like a winner is all about attitude. You must have self-confidence and believe that you are a winner. If you do not believe in yourself, it will come off in your attitude and actions. Do not get me wrong, I am not talking about being arrogant. It is all about confidence.

A winner's mentality is point blank, no excuses. The first time I heard someone say excuses are to just satisfy yourself, I did not understand it. If you think about it, this has some truth to it. When we make an excuse, we have to accept it first in our heart and mind before we voice it. Therefore, it is something that we agree with or sometimes tell ourselves why we did not do this or that. Never try to come up with excuses especially when the answer is, "I just quit or I just didn't know how." It is easy to come up with an excuse. We could think of one everyday not to go to work, right? To think and act like a winner, do not use excuses. Do not except excuses from others. It is a matter of people doing what they really want to do. It is amazing when it is something we really desire, we can get strength, find money, find a way, etc. Our self-will is very powerful. We must learn to tap into that power to achieve our goals.

You heard in times past that a winner never quits and a quitter never wins. That is pretty plain and simple. A quitter of course, cannot win because they gave up. To think like a winner, do not even think about quitting at all. A winner is thinking about completing the task no matter how long it takes. Learn to think in those terms. Even when new challenges arise, a winner attitude is still focused on getting to the reward. To a winner a challenge is an opportunity to learn something and to grow. Because challenges will arise, do not throw in the towel. Some people will not even take up a particular major in college because of one class they heard about. You must know that if others did it, so can you. Once you learn to face challenges and defeat challenges, this will provide you with unstoppable motivation.

Winners always believe they are going to succeed in the end. No matter what obstacles, you must have faith that you will win in the end. Winners just simply believe that they are going to attract good things towards them. This is called the Laws of Attraction. You are like a human magnet that can draw certain things towards you. You must learn to think good things and believe you will attract only good things. If you think negatively, you will attract negative things. Again, if you think you can do something, then you can. You just need to know your mind is very powerful and that you can attract good things if you believe. This is called faith, not a secret. Even though you are striving to achieve something, you must believe in your heart that you can achieve it.

Positive thinking is a mental attitude that reflects one's thoughts, words, and images that are conductive to success. It is a mental attitude that expects good and favorable results. A positive mind frame anticipates happiness, joy, health, and a successful outcome in every situation. Whatever your mind anticipates, it seeks. If you expect something, you will take action. When you take action, you get results.

Some people consider thinking positive nonsense. Some people will even brush you off if you encourage them the think positive or if you appear too positive. It is quite common to hear people say, "Think positive." Most people do not take these words seriously, as they do not know how powerful thinking positive can be. The positive thinking is the most important ingredient to thinking like a winner. Again, a winner expects good results. A winner expects to win. Even when the odds are not favorable, a winner expects to win or get high results. Apply your winning attitude to everything you do.

HAVE THE RIGHT ATTITUDE

YOU PROBABLY HAVE HEARD that the right attitude can take you a long way. Maybe you have even heard that your attitude will determine your altitude. Both of these statements are true. First impressions can leave a lasting impression on someone. Having a negative attitude can be toxic to others and you. Sometimes we can knock ourselves by having a negative attitude and poor body language. People provide opportunities for others simply based on their attitude. Something as simple as saying thank you can make a difference in how someone will view you. Think about someone that frowns all the time or toot their mouth up like they smile their own bad breath. Does anyone really want to be bothered with someone like that? Of course not! Simply smiling can make someone appear friendly and confident. The way we are viewed by others does matter to a certain degree when pursuing success. One of the main reasons is, no one has ever become successful alone. No one! This is true because we are all a product of our experiences and upbringing. So knowing this, we will have to consult others. We all will need others in our journey in becoming a success. People could make it hard for you or on the other hand help elevate you by making your way easy if they like you. I remember hearing a story about a young woman who was working the morning shift at a restaurant and she was very rude to a patron. Even though the patron did not complain, she thought within herself how negative the young woman was and preceded on to her job. Later that day, the patron who just happened to be an executive, had to interview some candidates for a position. Guess who comes in for an interview? The young woman from the restaurant from earlier that day. Even though she was qualified, the executive could not get over the attitude she had encountered earlier. A person's attitude is an extension of their personality. To see the true heart of a man is to see him when he faces adversity. His actions or non-actions will tell the heart of that man.

Having the right attitude or outlook on things is important. The right attitude is determined by how we think. This goes in conjunction with positive and negative thinking. If we let our personal attitudes and feelings towards others dictate our decisions, this will limit our networking ability. By doing this, we put limitations on our success.

When you send off a good vibe, you will receive good vibes in return. Remember, communication equals compensation. The better our personality, the more interesting, likable, and approachable you will appear. So be aware of your verbal and nonverbal vibes.

Everybody likes good attitudes or vibes. Enthusiasm is contagious! Have you ever noticed how people with a bubbly personality attract others? Confidence is an asset. Think about this, would you rather hang out with someone complaining all the time or someone that finds the light in darkness?

There is a difference between having a confident attitude and having an arrogant attitude. It is good to be confident. When you have confidence, you have faith in your ability. Being arrogant is a different story. Arrogant people feel as if they are entitled or better than others are. Arrogance can become aggressive and almost bullying behavior.

It is amazing how much you will achieve by just having the right attitude. It encourages rather than discourages. It motivates rather than interferes. It helps achieve rather than procrastinate. Having the right attitude makes everyone better. Everything is possible when you have a positive attitude to push you forward. Control the situation. My wife sometimes tells me, "Baby this person got on my nerves and got me all worked up." My answer is, "Baby they are your nerves, don't let them get on them." It is that simple, you do not have to let negative people drag you down. They will drain your positive spirit. Negative people are dream killers. Are these negative people worth you not living your dream?

Maintain Focus

Staying focused is very important when trying to achieve anything. It is crucial when trying to achieve your set goals. Getting focused usually is not a problem. Staying focused from so many distractions can get hard at time. Even though there will always be distractions around, you can still maintain focus. Of course, it is easier said than done because we live in a real world. Unexpected things will come up from time to time, but do not let these things detour you. Even though you have demands and responsibilities, you must never lose focus. Try to keep a clear mind and not get overloaded with other issues. Do not neglect other issues and do not get overloaded with them. Sometimes it will be other people's problems that can side track you. It is not that you do not care, but you just do not want to lose total focus. Ask yourself would they do it for you? Do not forget it is your dream, not theirs. So think about how badly you want it.

Keeping focus allows you to concentrate on exactly what you are trying to do. Always be focused and attentive, you will be able to evaluate your progress on a routine basis. This is simply a part of being organized. Being organized will help promote maintaining focus. When things are organized, it is easy to stay on track. Organization allows you to prioritize things on a constant basis. By doing this, you will get the most important things done first. This will also save time and break up each part down to small steps. All of this helps keep you on track.

Other ways to help stay on focus includes having a well-defined goal, planning ahead, and removing distractions. All of these help to promote focus in different ways, but having a well-defined goal is essential to maintain focus. This gives you a concrete specific target to focus on. This also prevents you from wasting a whole lot of time.

After setting a well-defined goal to focus on, it is good to create a well-defined plan. Even with a well-defined plan, it is good to always plan ahead. Planning will help save time in the event you get side tracked for a short period of time. When you do not plan it is just like when you do not leave to go somewhere ahead of time. If something comes up it will make you late.

If you leave early and something happens, you have that extra time to address it and move forward. With planning, if a distraction arises, you can address it quickly and not miss a beat. Planning will be discussed further in a later chapter. Finally, remove all distractions. This may not mean to physically move something, but avoid those things that slows or hinders your success. Distractions will definitely get you off focus. Sometimes this means avoiding negative individuals, certain conversations, certain events, etc. the main thing is to keep the focus.

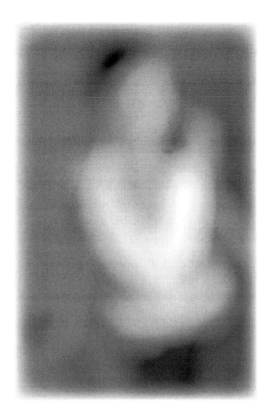

Some Ways to Stay Focused

1. Always have well defined goals that are reachable.
   Establish goals that are well defined with good guidelines are an essential key to success. We know it is important to write your goals down. Whenever you get distracted, read the goals and evaluate your progress. Remember with all of your goals, you must set timeframes to complete the goals.

2. Always have a plan to achieve the established goals.
   Having well defined goals is good, but having a plan of action is an essential key. A plan can identify how you can get from where you are to where you want to go. This will help promote focus!

3. Always prioritize your goals.
   Decide which tasks you should be working on first. Prioritization and organization will help allow you to stay focused. Some tasks will be more important than others will. Some tasks will be more urgent than others are. I have found out

that working on urgent tasks followed by tasks that have the greatest impact is best. Working on urgent tasks first allows you to get things done on time.

4. Always follow a routine.
   Having good habits and positive patterns is good for maintaining focus. Doing this, you will consistently get more done. As you continue to establish positive habits, you will be able to established timeframes, focusing and working on every task.

5. Always remove distractions.
   It would not be good to read a book while having the television or radio blasting. This will keep you distracted and ultimately slowing progress. To maintain focus you need to limit all distractions that you can control. If this means studying alone instead of with your best friend due to being together tends to become a laugh fest. Removing distractions and removing yourself from distractions will require some discipline. You must resist the temptation of all distractions and have the will power to do so.

6. Always use your support network.
   Always communicating with others in your field or someone that has achieved what you are trying to do. Find organization and clubs to join. Always find and keep a mentor. Not only will this be a helpful source of information, but also it promotes focus.

BE PERSISTENT

PERSISTENCE IS ANOTHER VERY important key to becoming successful. Many people fail at meeting their goals due to simply not being persistent. Persistence is a continuous driven perspective. Everyone has this self-driven will power, but must learn to tap into it. Persistence is sort of like pressing forward and seeing something through from start to finish. It simply is staying the course through everything that is required and anything that comes your way when trying to achieve a goal. No matter what, stick to it. If you have to take a test ten times, take it ten times. If you have to take a course three times, take it three times.

You must learn to be persistent no matter if you think you are moving slow or not moving at all. Simply never give up! Persist through the ups and the downs.

Being persistent is easier said than done. It is something we must train ourselves to do. We know about now that we must reprogram our minds. One thing we should think about is the rewards we will achieve if we stay persistent. Sort of keeping your eyes on the prize. It is good to picture yourself down the road living in your success or dream. Remember, if you can see it, you can be it. By thinking positively in this manner, it will help you continue to be driven. You must realize that the pain and obstacles will be worth it in the end. Plus, the pain and the obstacles do not last always.

Some people stop being persistent because success does not just happen all at once. It is easy to get displaced or to stay off track. It may appear that you are not getting anywhere or things are taking too long to take place. When these thoughts come, you must try to block out these thoughts immediately. If you entertain these ideas, you can become doubtful, fearful, and even give up. If someone entertains these thoughts too long, they can become stagnated. In other words, they begin to procrastinate. Again, it is best to avoid these feelings as quickly as they occur. Tell yourself, "I'm closer today than yesterday. " There will be times that you will be unsure about some things, but do not let this stop you from being productive. Continue to persist. Think about how bad do you want it. Think on how bad do you want to be successful. Think of how it could be life changing if you persist.

To be persistent in anything, one must learn to be disciplined. Discipline is simply doing something you need or want to do even if odds are against you. Being disciplined concerning small things will help propel you to meeting your goals and become successful. Sometimes you may have to take one hour at a time, but keep striving. Do not worry if you do not know how something may go or turn out. It is good to stay on track by staying productive and moving forward.

Persistent is not to give up when striving to reach your goals. It simply means hanging in there when things get tough or look dim. No matter what, we must learn to keep moving forward, being persistent. To be highly successful or have a business, you have to be persistent.

A lot of businesses and ventures failed due to lack of persistence. Sometimes we are not persistent because things may get hard or look dim like it is not going to happen. Most people eventually give up. We must get in the mind frame that no matter how dull things may seem, we must continue to push forward. Think about it, if you do something repeatedly over and over again, eventually you are going to get better. This is being persistent. It is hard for some to take these small failures until they succeed. Just think about it as a learning process. If you try to pass a test 100 times, and it takes you passing it on the 101st time, then do it. Each time you took the test during the 100 times you began to realize not to do it a particular way, because you got the question wrong. You get closer and closer each time you attempt. The thing about it is, most people give up. You do not have to give up! Just wait it out and see things through. See things through. There is a scripture that says those that wait upon the Lord shall renew their strength. We must develop this patience to see things through. I recall another scripture stating the Lord is a rewarder of them that diligently seek him. A lot of times people start a business and expect things to happen over night or for things to happen like it did for someone else. We have all heard the old saying "you got to crawl before you walk." This is true. We must realize that our crawl may take longer than someone else's crawl. It could be shorter. Just know this so you will not get caught up evaluating yourself by someone else's success or achievements. It may take you 5 years to finish college. It may take someone else 3 years. Evaluating yourself by someone else can cause you to lose focus. It can make you feel like you are not getting anywhere. Everybody moves at their own pace. Again, your crawl could just take a little bit longer.

Going through the ups and downs of persistence can be challenging if you let it. You know there will be those who say, "Well it hasn't happened yet." You will even get doubtful yourself and think, "Well it hasn't happened. It doesn't look like it's going to happen." I know we all heard this one, "you're wasting your time." You have to put those thoughts to rest. If you honestly get prepared, do your homework, and give 110 percent, there is no reason why you should not press forward when trying to achieve goals or dreams. Staying focused on the results will help put the doubts to rest. Evaluate your progress. Evaluate how far away you are from reaching your goal. Go over all that you have learned. Again, take it all as a learning experience. Learn everything from all your small failures. Benefit from them. Learn what doesn't work so you will know what does.

In being persistent, you will always need encouragement. To get encouragement, you must surround yourself with others that are open-minded. Sometimes you may have to encourage yourself. A lot of times people start off with us, but if things do not happen quickly, they fall off. Always remember, that it is your dream. It is you vision! It is your goal! Everybody is not going to share your vision. Does this mean the vision should stop? Of course not! Think about Noah Arch. He was persistent even though he probably was laughed at. When you step out and enter into an area none of your peers has gone before, they are going to think you are strange. Most people do what their peers do. So stepping out can sometimes brings about friction. Again, realize it is your dream, so it is for you to stick with. You have to decide if this is what you want. You may be taking baby steps at times, but see your visions through. One thing for sure, if you persist each day, you will be one-step closer than yesterday. For example, think about someone going to school. A 10th grader may think it is taking forever to finish school. Actually if he or she looked behind himself or herself, they would realize that they have already completed many years and only have a few left. Some students get that close to completion and quit. We know at this point that a quitter never wins. Also, a winner never quits. So be a winner!

We have already established hard work pays off. Do not worry if things are going slower than you would like. Just know that the race is not given to the swift or the battle to the strong, but unto the one that endures unto the end. We all know the story about the rabbit and turtle racing. Even though the rabbit was faster, he did not win in the end. The turtle did not give up and was persistent.

Persistence is what makes success stick like glue. Persistence is the vehicle that gets us across the bridge to success. If you persist and do not give up, success is guaranteed. It is going to happen. No matter how often we attempt something, it is persistence that will help things finally pay off. The bible even lets us know that the Lord is a rewarder of them that diligently seek Him. We have often heard if we seek, we shall find. Notice it did not say how long you would have to seek, but it did guarantee that we shall find. Persistence is what gets you there. In addition, we have heard that if you knock, it shall be open unto you. Now, it did not say how many times you would have to knock. We have also heard that if we ask, it shall be given unto us. Again, it did not say how long. Many times, we are right there at the place we should be, but too often we give up too soon. Anything worth having is worth waiting for. Doubt sets in if something does not happen as we had planned, but we must be persistent and stick to it. Some people start a business and they expect it to do wonders overnight. After sticking with it a few months, they give up. Some things take longer than others do, but if you have prepared as you have been taught, things will eventually turn for the positive.

Some people start and quit everything they do. Someone that does this does not have the right mind frame. Every time things get hard, it does not mean to start making excuses and quit. When things get challenging, that is an opportunity to brainstorm. We know so many people that start and quit stuff every week, every few months, etc. Whatever the case may be, we all know people that start things and all of a sudden, here they go again. We have known people to work a few months and it appears that they are about to achieve, but then they lose the drive. We all know these people, right? I know it because this used to be me. I would start businesses every few months. I am selling at the flea market one day, the next week I am selling cd's. Many people are doing this right now. I had to tell myself that I have to stick to something. You have to realize that you have to see something through. Once you target your goal, dream, or vision, you must stick to it. You cannot jump around. You have to get organized and prepared. When this is happening, the person is not yet committed to his or her goal or dream. Your goal may be to lose weight. Most people do not keep the weight off because they are not persistent with what they have started. We must learn to be persistent and stick it out. Learn everything about what you are trying to do. What if all inventors would have just quit researching, producing, and testing their products? Think about the light bulb. Think about everything. Did you know that some items are tested thousands of times before they are perfected? Inventors take every failure as a learning experience. You must learn to do the same. Tell yourself, "Okay that didn't work." At that point, you know not to do that anymore. We must learn to keep working at things. Failure is not an option.

You can be persistent. We show persistence in our daily living. I find a lot of times we are more persistent towards someone else's dream. We are not even persistent towards our own dreams at times. Think about that. The company you work for is a way you are probably helping someone fulfill their dreams. If you worked for a company for 5 years, you have been persistent at coming to work for 5 years. So why aren't we persistent when it comes to our goals and dreams? There should not be any doubt on whether you can be persistent or not. You have already proven you have been for years. Some people are persistent in negative ways. For example, some drug addicts will hit the street every night hunting drugs and so forth. So obviously, they could be persistent enough to go to work 5 days a week. You see persistence is mind over matter. It is all about how badly do you want something. The bottom line is this; people do what they want to do. It is as simple as that. I knew a guy who could never find a way to put in a job application, but he could always find a way to go to the malls, clubs, and Mardi Gras parades. You see, when we focus on the end results, we make something happen. Somehow, we find a way. Even if one ride cannot do it, we call someone else. Even if the other one cannot, we stay persistent until we find a way. The challenge is to turn this around and apply it to our dreams and goals. Let's look at the outcome. Again, for instance, finding a job.

If the person focuses in on "I don't have a way", "they're probably not hiring", it is a slim chance they are going to take action. On the other hand, if the focus is put on, I am going to find a way up there and when I get that job, I am going to have some extra spending money will promote action. Focus on the positive. Focus on the results. Yes, simply think about the rewards. The rewards are enough to give you a push. Think on how happy you will be when you reach your goal. Look at how it will impact your life. If achieving a goal will help you gain something, focus on it. If it will help you get a house, pin a picture of the dream house on the refrigerator as a reminder. Focusing on the rewards and how achieving your goals will change your life will help you persist through rough times. This will help you look beyond all the hard work or how challenging things might be. All you know is you are going to do it because the rewards are going to allow you to live the life you want to live. Another example is college. The focus should be on getting that degree not "I'm not good at math." The focus should be whatever it takes to get to my goal of getting that degree. The stronger your focus is, the easier things become.

PLAN FOR SUCCESS

YOU SHOULD PLAN FOR everything. It could be simply planning to go to the grocery store. When you establish a plan, you get an underlining sense of what is ahead. Planning should be applied to every area of our life. This is forward thinking. If you want to go on a vacation, you must plan it. The same goes for success, retirement, financial freedom, and anything you can think of. You could even plan to plan. One thing for sure, after you establish a goal you should make a plan.

Your goal is set. Now, you need to make a plan to achieve that goal. What exactly is a plan or should I say what is planning? Planning is basically preparing a sequence of action steps to achieve a specific goal. Planning is almost more important than having the goal itself. Without a plan, you will be unorganized and waste a lot of time. On the other hand, if you have an effective plan, you will be able to make progress with ease. Also, by having a plan you will be able to evaluate your progress on a regular basis. Notice that a plan has action steps. Remember, you must take action and work the plan!

A plan is sort of like a map or guide. When you follow the instructions, you should end up at the targeted destination. Think about a recipe of your favorite cake. If you take the same steps the bakery did, you should be able to make the same cake. This is simply the same when trying to achieve a particular goal. Of course, there are many ways to make a cake, but the message is to have a plan to follow. Without the recipe, you may end up with a biscuit.

Planning allows you to leverage time. Taking out the time to plan each day will improve your productivity. Giving yourself a few moments to target what you are going to do will allow you to prioritize things and save time. For example, some things could possibly be grouped together. When you make a to-do list, some errands could be done together at one store. This is why so many people love Wal-Mart. People save time by getting their clothes, medication, and food at one store. By just taking out the time to plan, you lay out the objectives or outcomes you desire, getting them done quickly. Without a plan, you will be unorganized. Also, you will waste time and money. Your time is priceless. Time is something you cannot get back.

Planning will also help eliminate bad habits and the fear of failure. If you stick to the plan, you will decrease procrastination. A well-prepared plan will decrease your fears by providing a constructive guide that you can see. Planning is essential to success. Your plan is the road map. Think about trying to drive in a foreign country without a map. This is a good example of trying to become successful without a plan. A good planner will have a Plan A, Plan B, and C. This simply indicates that this planner is thinking ahead. It also shows determination to reach the set goal.

Steps to Plan for a Successful Future

1. Go to a quiet area where you can focus. Just go somewhere you will not have distractions. Some people may feel comfortable at a café, a beach, or simply at home. This involves personal preference.

2. Reflect on your life thoroughly. What are your talents? What are your gifts? What do you want to be in the future? What is your passion? What would you desire to do even if you weren't paid for it.

3. Write it down! By this time, this should be automatic in your head. You could start a notebook. Most of the people who have achieved their dreams took the first step toward achieving them; they wrote them down. At this point, you may not even know where to start, but still write something down.

4. Plan a route to get there. Write down whatever it will take to reach your dream. Sometimes this may require research. In addition, it may require help from others. Just make sure that your plan is a workable plan. Do not start too high that you cannot work the plan.

5. Put notes where you can see it and remind yourself of your goals. Post it on your refrigerator, mirror, computer, etc. The main thing is, you need to see it often. When you see it, you will continue to work towards the set goal.

6. Work your plan. Put it into action by following the route to your dream. It may mean adjusting a lot of things in your life, but it will be worth it one day. Just ask tennis great Serena Williams. Ask any successful person.

7. Start a savings account or some form of investment account.

Things to consider:

1. Make sure the goal(s) you are working on is something you really want, not just something that sounds good. Your goal must be something achievable by you. Notice that I said by you. Your goal may be achievable but if you lack certain ingredients such as funds, it could stop the project. So make sure, your goal(s) are always achievable.

2. Develop goals in different areas of life. This will make you more well rounded. Growing financially but not mentally and spiritually is not good. If you grow financially but remain the same or below in your mental state, it will affect your financial security.

3. Write your goal in the positive instead of the negative. Always write or speak in the positive. Think like a winner. Talk and write like a winner. This shows that you believe what you are writing.

4. Write your goal out in complete detail. Be very specific! Include all details concerning your goal and plan.

5. Aim high! By all means, make sure your goal is high enough. You do not want to aim too high or too low. Go higher than you went before. Once you reach that, go even higher.

You can create a mission or goal statement. This could be the driving force and purpose behind everything that you are planning to do. You know at this point to write it down. You can break it down to weeks, months, years, etc. When listing your goals, you must consider things you will have to give up and any sacrifices you will need to make. Your plan should reflect this. Once you have your mission, plan, and goal, create a binder to review it periodically. Read your mission and goals often.

DEVELOP GOALS FOR SUCCESS

PLANNING IS SORT OF like a blue print. A plan is a scheme, program, or method worked out beforehand for the accomplishment of an objective. It could be proposed, tentative project or course of action. This systematic arrangement of elements or objectives are outlined. We know at this point, you should always plan before starting on your journey to success. Again, would you go on a trip without planning? Of course not! A plan can be used as a guideline and tool to evaluate progress. Planning and setting goals go together, but they are slightly different. Planning identifies the main tasks, allocates a time scale to each task, and allows for contingencies. A goal is the purpose toward which an endeavor is directed. It is the set objective to be accomplished. Goals can be short term and long term.

Goal setting is very powerful. It is very important to set goals to measure progress towards success. Also, if we do not have something to target, we would just be going in circles. Setting goals is a powerful tool for thinking about where you are trying to go. By knowing exactly what you want to achieve, you can focus more on a specific matter. This saves lots of time and cuts down on procrastination. It also helps motivate you to turn your vision of the future into reality.

We all set goals at some point in our life. It may be something as small as wanting to pass a test or wanting to buy a dream car. The difference with highly successful people is they set their goals, re-evaluate the goals, achieve the goals, and reset new goals. This includes professional athletes, business leaders, etc. Once you get in the habit of setting goals for yourself and conquering them, you will improve in almost every area of your life. You will gain long-term visions and immediate motivation to take action to reach towards the set goal. It is easy to evaluate your progress and to get back on track when you stray because the end result does not change. The end result of course is to reach the set goal. Always set clear and well-defined goals. Brainstorm and come up with goals that you truly desire to accomplish. This is important because if you do not really want to do it from the start, you will quit. Whatever goal you set, you have to view it as something that gives you a pleasurable feeling when you reach it. Even if the task is something hard, never view it as unpleasurable. Visualize how great you would feel once you achieve the goal.

After you come up with a clear goal and know where you are trying to go, write it down. This is something you must get used to doing. Write them down! This may sound so unimportant, but it must be done. We all are guilty of setting a goal in our mind and it stays right there, in our mind. A dream or idea is something simply in your mind. When you write it down, it is out of your mind and becomes reality. You can look at it, post it, and touch it. Write your goal down and aim towards reaching it. Remember, you are reprogramming your mind.

Make up a to do lists daily to work towards achieving the set goal. Remember to ask yourself what have I done today and each day to reach my goal. By taking this active approach daily, you will get closer to achieving the set goal. It is very important to set timelines for your goals. For example, if you have a goal you want to complete by the end of the year, have a short-term goal by the sixth month of the year. This way you can measure how far you have gotten and how close you are to achieving the goal. Setting a deadline is critical to prevent you from procrastinating. Setting a deadline is also a motivator to force you to take action and to constantly evaluate progress.

You can set goals for every area of your life, but it is good to focus only on a few goals at a time to maintain focus. Some people can focus on more things than others can. Always know your strengths and situations. Many people set personal goals only. To be successful, you must learn to set goals in several areas short-term and every area of your life long-term. Every aspect of you should be considered. Have you ever thought about career goals, financial goals, spiritual goals, family goals, physical goals, public service goals, etc? As you see, you can set goals in many areas in your life. It is strictly up to you. I have learned that it is important to set short-term goals to experience small victories along the way to a long-term goal. This is important because you do not want to feel like a goal is taking forever to reach.

You should know at this point, setting goals is very important to being successful. This is something that many people take lightly. I know I did. Most of the time we think in our minds about what goals we want to achieve. After that, we confirm within ourselves, yes I want to do this or that. The excitement is there and we are off to conquer. Initially, we stay with it but slack up. Many times, we start with the intention of reaching our goal, but become consumed with other things. A perfect example is losing weight. We may start full force but lose focus to something else. As previously stated, to keep focus, it is best to write your goals down. Personally, I used to set goals all the time. The only problem was I was setting the goals only in my mind. Think about all the goals you have set in your life and you simply forgot about them. After going to seminars, reading books, and listening to tapes, they all said to do the same thing. They said to write your goals down. Therefore, I thought what is writing down my goals going to do. Writing it down is not going to help me achieve anything is what I told myself. I decided to write down a few goals. It felt like it was more reachable. By looking at my goals on paper, I could re-evaluate my progress each week. It is important to see it, so you can stay on track to reach your goals. Now, do you see how easily your dreams become achievable and realistic?

I got excited about goal setting. I began to set goals, both short term and long term. I wrote goals concerning everything, especially finances. My brother lived next door, and I went over and said, "Take a look at how I'm going to make a million dollars." He listened as always. I showed him how I was going to save about $2,500 of my tax return. From that $2,500, I would turn it in to $5,000 and so forth. I had the figures mapped out to a million dollars. After all of that, he asked how was I going to do it (make the money). I told him, that was my only problem. Actually, I did not know how I was going to do it, but I knew that whatever it took I was going to do it. To answer, what you are thinking, no I am not a millionaire, but I did save $2,500 from my income tax that year. My point is, you must set goals and re-evaluate them. Even if you do not know how you are going to do it at the time you set your goals. You do not want to start by saying "I want to save a million dollars." The reason is if you set the amount too high, it will seem too far away. You will eventually get burned out. Start with something reasonable like $1,000 in the next 6 months. Everyone knows his or her limit. Some people may try to save $5,000 in six months. Set your goals in $100, $500, $1,000, $2,500 or $5,000 increments. For example, after you reach $1,000, you could set your goal to reach $2,000. It is up to you to set your goal. Never set it so high that you cannot seem to reach your 6-month goal. It is important not to set it too high, because you need to experience reaching your goal and feel the satisfaction of winning. Once you reach your goal over and over again, you will immediately reset your goal and strive to go higher. Your ultimate goal is up to you. There is no limit on this. Once you reach your ultimate goal, you can invest it in a way that it makes money for you.

What do you do with your tax return? Do you buy new clothes? Did you realize this is the perfect time to save? Yes, save it! I would hear people young and old talking around tax time about how they got these large refunds. A few months pass by and then they are in the same situation as before. Most people spend all of their refund without saving any for the latter part of the year when there is so much to do. In the summer and fall, it would be perfect to have this money to go on trips, etc. If you got $3,000 back, saved for a few months, you really could throw a nice Fourth of July barbeque. The refund could also be used as a down payment for a house. We must learn how to get the most value out of our money. It could be used to jump start a savings account. It could be placed in an IRA account for retirement. Think about this, if you are averaging $3,000 a year on refunds and you save $2,000 of that for the next ten years you have saved $20,000 with no effort. No effort at all! This is without including interest. Money compounds! The sooner you start saving the better.

MAKE GOOD DECISIONS

MAKING DECISIONS IS NOT difficult. We make hundreds of simple decisions each day. It could be simple as deciding what to eat or wear. Some decisions take more thought. Simple decisions do not require much thought. Most of the time with these decisions, we have established opinions before we even decide. Even though these decisions are easy to make, there are some decisions that should always be thought about. Making good decisions or choices is an important key to success. Making good choices can propel you towards success faster. On the other hand, making bad choices will affect your progress. Some bad choices may ultimately prevent you from ever being successful. If you think about it, all aspects of life are about making choices. We are faced with making all sorts of choices our entire life. Think back when you were a teenager and you had to make a choice on whether to engage in some sort of bad deed with other teenagers. Whether you agree or not, the choice is put on the table. For whatever reason a decision is made whether it is right or wrong. The key in this is very simple cause and effect. We learn this early in life but never apply this to our daily life. Remember the rule is each action has an effect. Knowing this, whatever decision we make has effects. This is important when striving to be successful. Whatever decisions you make today will affect your tomorrow. All of the choices you make can help you or hurt you. Therefore, you learn to practice good decision-making techniques. Learn to use these techniques daily. When you learn how to evaluate things and make better decisions, you experience success. This is because, you are taking away the risk when you make decisions. You are making an informed decision. When you make an inform decision you are fully aware of all the details. By doing this, it limits your chances of failure.

When making an informed decision, you must gather information. You are unlimited on what resources to use when gathering information. It could be as simple as asking someone or searching on-line. The main thing is you need to gather information to be informed. After you gather the information, you need to evaluate the pros and cons. This simply means to look at how the decision will affect you. Then identify any negative consequences of the decision. The decision must be thought out thoroughly. It is good to seek advice from others. An outside person can give a nonjudgmental view on the pros and cons. Sometimes you may overlook a specific point. When you seek out advice, make sure you consult well-rounded individuals. This needs to be someone that knows how to analyze information.

At this point, you need to review the pros and cons directly towards you personally. When doing this, you must be honest with yourself. Know what your strengths and weaknesses are. Know what you can manage or not. This will save you time and hardships. One of the main reasons people fell at things is because it was not in their destiny. If you honestly know something is not for you, do not waste time running in circles. That is why being true to yourself is important in decision making because you already have core behaviors.

Once you have done these steps, you are ready to make an informed decision on any situation. When you make informed decisions and things do not go exactly as planned, you have a sense of dignity because you were aware of the possibilities from the start. This does not give you a feeling of failure, but the motivation to re-evaluate the situation. Most often, when you make informed choices, you will make good decisions. Of course, when you make uninformed decisions you are just trying to be lucky. Success is not based on luck, but sound decisions. So remember, the decisions we make today will affect our tomorrow. This applies when striving to be successful also. So always, make informed decisions for the best results.

ACQUIRE KNOWLEDGE AND EDUCATION

EDUCATION IS VERY IMPORTANT to your success. It is basic human right. Even though you have the right to access information, it is up to you to do this. The return on education is priceless. Learning is an essential to becoming a success. The more you know, the further you will go. Another one of my sayings is, "Communication rules the nation." I am not necessarily saying what type of studies is required, but you must be willing to gain knowledge and information. You must always keep that burning desire to learn new things. If you never learn anything new, you become stagnated in mental growth. When you obtain knowledge, you receive immediate progress towards your goals. It can be just that fast or it could be a process. One thing for sure is, once you gain information, no one can take it away from you. Is college good? Of course, it is, but you will not learn how to be highly successful in college. Lots of time, the person teaching you does not even have real world experiences on the subject matter they teach. For example, your business professor may never have owned a business. Your finance professor may not even have a good financial record. So, when you think about education, do not just think about a college education. Start looking at education and learning as a life long journey. Think about it, you have been learning since you were born until now. So, always continue to seek opportunities to learn and build upon them. Just like when you scooted, then crawled, and then walked as a baby. From now on look at learning as a never-ending venture. When we view education and learning this way, we desire to explore more. Education impacts your human development and economic growth. This is true when trying to be successful. You now realize success does not just happen by luck. If you are better prepared in a specific area, it is a great chance you will master it.

You should never stop seeking opportunities to learn. Never! There is something out there to know that can improve you and your life. I am not even saying go to college your entire life. I am saying even after high school, even after college, even after graduate school, there is something else to learn. Even if you feel like college is not for you, there are still learning opportunities. Going to seminars, community centers, articles, websites, etc will help you gain a wealth of information. Talking to others in a field or subject is helpful also. The key is obtaining knowledge and information. If someone knows how to do something you do not, ask him or her so you can advance. It does not matter if you have to learn it from a child. We should never stop seeking out knowledge and understanding. I remember as a child in school if I did not know something I would seek out help from whomever. I can recall getting help from my two younger sisters in Math and English. One was good at Math and the other at English. The point is, we must seek out help and gain knowledge from others who have the knowledge of that subject matter. Successful people understand the power of knowledge, whether it is gaining knowledge or recognizing the knowledge of others. The main objective is to reach a higher level than before, to gain more knowledge and understanding than before. After obtaining knowledge, you have to utilize it. The knowledge is no good if it is not applied. Even if you go to college and get a degree, you still have to get out and apply it. We all know someone who has a talent or knowledge that is not utilizing it.

College is very important for being successful because we live in an information age. A college degree increases your chances of being successful. Some college is better than no college. College also helps prepare you for social and culture diversity by dealing with different personalities. It helps equip you for the world and the job market. Any preparedness is better than none. Think about this, you are working for someone that knew something you did not. You are working for someone who started his or her own business. Whether it was the idea to create a company, have a plan to move up, or whatever. They found out what it took to go to a higher level. Having a college education looks good on job applications and even when trying to get a loan. Knowledge is very powerful no matter what or how you obtain it. Once we know something, nobody can make us go back to our old ways of thinking. It really saddens me to see all the opportunities the youth have and they do not utilize them. Many people gave their lives for all of us to have the opportunity at an education. Knowing this, it should be taken advantage of. Learn everything you can about what you are trying to accomplish. Learn it from A to Z. Master it! Learn it in and out.

BUILD A STRONG NETWORK

ANOTHER IMPORTANT WAY TO gain knowledge is networking. Networking is essential in today's fast-paced world. There are no reasons today why we should not have access to information and informative professionals. Everybody knows someone that does something. For instance, you may not know how to work on a car, but you probably know someone you could ask questions about repairing a car. What this is letting you know is that even if you do not have knowledge of something, if you have access to it through someone else, you can benefit from it. Today we have access to many things through the Internet, books, and other things. You may not know anything about a subject or have a degree in a field, but networking will give you access to everything. You may not become a doctor, but you have access to the same information he or she does. You may not know how to build a deck, but you have access to learn how.

There are many places to network. Social events are a good place to network. It may be at a ball game, church event, or a birthday party. There are many social events you could network at. You should take advantage of these opportunities. You never know who knows who or who knows someone that does certain things that you are interested in. By talking to people positively about your field of interest, you could get great referrals. Each time you gain a little more knowledge on a subject matter. Let's say for example, you are at a gathering and you are interested in starting a daycare. It is good to mingle and find out what other people do. Even if they do not own a daycare, they may say, "My sister owns one of those." Just by talking to one person you will have access to everyone they know. This is so important to success. You must get in the frame of mind of taking something good away from everyone you meet. Using a networking approach, you have access to everything, which takes limits off of reaching your goals.

What is networking? We network every day to some degree. It may be small or great, but we have a circle of individuals that we get general information from. Networking is simply establishing beneficial relationships between two or more parties to gain, to share, or support and establish information on a particular subject matter. Networking is a part of communication. Networking is a common business practice. When striving to be successful, networking can propel you forward very quickly. It is a saying concerning it is not about what you know, but who you know. This is very true. Creating a strong network could save you time and money. Being reluctant to network could cost you time and money. Being reluctant to network could equal failure. We have heard the old saying that there is power in numbers. This is very true in a lot of ways, especially when you have more people to ask questions from. This gives you a greater chance of getting the answer.

If you call someone today with questions concerning a project, it is a good chance they will be able to give you some information about it or make a referral. It is very common that we all know somebody that knows somebody, right. In today's society, knowledge or know how is abundant everywhere. The key is to get to that knowledge. Everybody we come across has mastered something. It may be small or great. Some people have mastered how to be lazy and if you are looking to be that, they can tell you how. On the other hand, if you are trying to do something, someone somewhere has information on it to share. Just like you are knowledgeable about something. There are others who have an abundance of information willing to share just for the asking.

You may know someone that can do something you cannot. It may be a skill, get in touch with a contact, get access to a place, etc. You must determine who these individual are and seek assistance. If you are a novice to investing, wouldn't you think it would be a good idea to consult with others that invest or a financial advisor? It does not matter if you can count to ten, if you network in this area and gain knowledge from someone else; you are just as powerful as they are in that area. Think about it, most of our service calls; we hire individuals for their knowledge or know how. We call the mechanic because he has the knowledge to fix the car. We call the electrician, because he understands wiring. Just imagine you had an electrician in your network. You could call at 8 pm just for information or even come out to provide a service. This makes you a more effective person. You will be able to be more productive than others. The reason is you have faster and better access. Think about this, if you had a friend as a lawyer, it would be easy to pick up the phone on a Saturday night and ask advice on a matter. Someone else would have to wait until Monday to phone a lawyer and still may not get an appointment for two weeks. Now, do you see how powerful networking can be? The second person that had to wait to call an attorney on Monday wasted a lot of time. Lost time is something that can never be made up. Also, the person that called the lawyer on Saturday is already moving forward to the next thing.

To me, networking is sort of like having eight arms like an octopus compared to only having two. There is no limit to networking. Networking makes the world a small place. In some form, we all affect one another directly or indirectly.

When you network, your opportunities, knowledge, and socialization skills grow. When trying to become successful, who you know can help you greatly. Lots of time, your way will be made easy because of this. The days of becoming highly successful without networking are gone. Networking is important to having success. This will make you stronger as a person. You will be able to build a strong team or network. This is a good way to increase knowledge and decrease fear of failure. You should definitely build a strong network in your area of interest, but do not forget to think outside the box. You should also network and communicate with others that are not directly connected to your field also. For example, it does not matter if your field is plumbing or not. It is good to network with others also in other areas. You never know when you will get the call asking did you know of a plumber. Also, you will one day need one or simply need some sort of information.

Networking opportunities are everywhere. Networking is more than just greeting people. You can develop a step-by-step plan to build beneficial relationships to help promote success. Know the specific type of person or group you need to focus on networking with. Determine where you will have the greatest chance of meeting professionals of your targeted interest. Of course, anyone can be a source of information, but you want your network to be strong as possible. I try to network with people smarter than me. When you do this, you gain their expertise on issues that you may have weaknesses in. Do take in consideration that everyone has something to give. You may not have to consult some people as much as others. The larger your networking resources are, the more knowledge you will be able to access. Even if the individual you network with does not know something, they will ask someone within their networking pool. When you establish a networking relationship, make sure you keep that relationship ongoing. Always follow up with associates. When people know that you appreciate them, they will be more willing to help you again. During the holidays, it is good to send a card. There are many ways to keep relationships established. It is recommended that you maintain all your strong associations.

Learn Money Management

Once successful, it is important to maintain it. Knowing how to manage money is essential to long-term success. It takes a while to accumulate, but it can be gone in a few seconds. It may seem like a lot as you look at your balance, but it could be gone with just a few withdrawals. Have you ever noticed when you break a $20 dollar bill, it seems to disappear? We wonder, "What did I do with the rest of that twenty?" Just like this can happen with a twenty-dollar bill, it could happen with a large amount. For a matter of fact, it can happen even at a greater rate with larger sums of money. The reason is once you break the $20 you do not notice the change as much. What I mean is, you do not monitor where every dime is going. No, it does not disappear; it is you that spent the rest of it. On the larger scale, if you had a thousand dollars you are more prone not to watch it closely because you think, "I'm a long way from zero." By feeling like this, people get relaxed and spend freely. The more we have, the more likely the less we monitor it (example $20). The less we have we watch it closer because it is near zero (example $5). Have you ever noticed the less we have, the more we focus on our needs only? For instance if you only had ten dollars to last you all week, you will most likely use it for gas or something vital. On the other hand, when we have a lot we normally spend freely.

Start noticing the foreigners that come over to the U.S. with practically nothing and in a few short years, we have to work for them. Of course, they receive have some perks, but they literally monitor every penny. Think about how our Chinese brothers and sisters manage money. How many Chinese people have you ever seen driving a Cadillac? How many have you ever seen eating at the expensive popular restaurants? How many have you ever seen in the big department store? My point is this, we can learn a lot from other cultures on how to manage money. My point is, lots of time we focus on wants more than necessity. Many foreigners focus only on needs. I am not saying never get your wants, but realize that many times we are simply being wasteful. Think about it, how many things this month did you purchase that you actually needed? How many things did you actually just want? The main things of course are food, clothing, shelter, and health needs. Think about all the other money we waste each year. What if we had saved just half of it? Many foreigners see us as being a wasteful nation, which we are in a lot of ways. It makes me think about each year we go out and buy all these Christmas gifts for kids, then two weeks later they do not even have an interest in them.

You cannot buy everything you see. Many of the times, we feel the urge to buy wants because we are unconsciously programmed. Your mind is very powerful. The scholars of the world know this, so they launch as mass media at us each day to persuade us to spend, spend, and spend. We see billboards, watch commercials on TV, hear commercials on the radio, etc. Advertising agencies program us to what they feel is acceptable or popular. Some commercials give the impression that if you try the product, it will work. Advertising is done in this manner to make us give into our wants. The challenge is to find a balance. Once something is programmed in your mind, it can associate feelings. Sometimes we like buying things to show off to others. This is the wrong way of thinking when aiming at long-term success. You should not buy a $70,000 car to try to impress someone else. They are not going to help with your car payment, so why purchase something to try to impress someone else. Do things to impress yourself only. It is wise to live modestly. It is good to budget. Sam Walton, the founder of Wal-Mart once said, "It's not about how much you make but about how much you keep." If you make $300 a week, but have a $400 a week lifestyle, you will never get ahead. If you make $60,000 a year but you only have $1,000 saved at t he end of the year, you might as well have made minimum wage. We must learn to be disciplined. You control the money. It does not it control you. Some people feel like if they cash their check they have to spend it. You must have discipline and self-control. You have to take control of your finances.

Some people make minimum wage but they have a place to live and such. They are able to make it because they do not waste their money on things that they do not need. For example, if you have two teachers that make the same amount of money, why is it that one may live in a shack and other a nice home? They can have the same education and everything, but some people manage their money better than others do. It does not matter what professional level you are on, if you do not manage your money right, you will continue to struggle. You can be a doctor making a six-figure salary and struggle due to mismanagement of your funds. Again, it is important to live within your means to try to avoid financial distress.

There are four types of incomes. To even have a chance, you will need to have at least one form of income. To be highly successful, you will need to have more than one form of income. The more forms of income you have increases your speed to success. Listed below are the definitions of the four forms of income.

1. <u>Earned Income</u>: (also referred to as linear income) This is where there is a direct correlation between your time and income - They are directly connected. In other words, you are trading your time for dollars - You work 8 hours, you are paid for 8 hours….You do not work- You don't get paid! Examples: A job or income endeavor requiring your time & involvement or any business (usually service businesses) in which you must be there in order to operate.

2. <u>Residual Income</u>: This is income that you gain by doing something correctly once, and then reaping the financial profits repeatedly without any further effort on your part. Examples: royalties, a percentage of a previously sold product that has a re-occurring income i.e., insurance, a monthly membership product/ service, real estate property returning rental income, and weekly or monthly subscriptions. Also being involved in legitimate network marketing program is a proven method that many have used to build a solid residual income.

3. <u>Leveraged Income</u>: Income that you gain in conjunction with the combined efforts of others. Examples: A team, sub-affiliates in your affiliate programs, or your employees. Others actually work to generate income towards your bottom

line. You can multiply repeatedly. That is the power of leveraged income…it is greater than you are alone…it multiplies your efforts!

4. Passive Income: Any type of income that does not require your time (or very little of it) in order to sustain. Examples: Investments, high interest bearing accounts, and legitimate network marketing.

SAVE TO GET AHEAD

SAVING IS IMPORTANT TO get ahead. This is also important to become successful and to stay successful. It is important to adopt this way of thinking because you can become unsuccessful very fast by not following this. If you have abundance or not, it is good to think about a rainy day. It does not matter if you are a doctor or a store clerk, everyone should always put something to the side in order to get ahead. We all have heard of individuals that come into large sums of money and they lose it all. One of the reasons is, they do not put anything up for a later time. This can happen to anyone. It does not matter whether if you have a PhD or you are a D student. You can work for 50 years and have nothing to show for it. What we do today or save today will determine our tomorrow. Do not get me wrong and think I am saying to save every penny or try to obtain the whole world. What I am expressing is that we must think about getting ahead and tomorrow. We should not just think about the present only. Just thinking about the now is more of an immediate gratification. When we consider our current actions in anything in relation to the future, we are considering others, also. It is better to have something saved than to need something and have nothing at all.

There are many ways to save funds. Most ways are common. Some choose to work a little extra or have a part time job. Starting a small business or smart investments is another way to save to get ahead also. Know what way you want to go. The main thing is that you get started.

Live within your means. Simply do not over spend. Get what you can afford or get just below what you can afford. Because society is very material oriented does not mean you have to be. Some people make a very good salary, but live way above their means. For example, if you make $100,000 a year, but you have a $125,000 lifestyle, you are not going to be able to save. That is why it is important to pay attention to your expenses so they will not get out of hand. Again, it does not matter what you make, if you do not have anything at the end of the year to show for it. Working is already stressful, so wouldn't it be only smart to get something out of the deal in the end. Anybody with common sense should know by now that you cannot rely on retirement alone from employers.

To get ahead you must save! It is imperative to save in the times we live in. Some people do not save because they do not have self-control. I should say they do not have enough discipline of self-will. Some people do not save due to the fear of someone else may benefit from it if something ever happens to him or her. I once worked with a guy that felt this way. I was very surprised! He stated that nobody was going to benefit off him. By the way, this guy was married with kids. I listened in disbelief and thought if he died, he would not know if they used his burial money for his burial. He would not know anything. There are many reasons why people do not save. You know for whatever reason you may not save or save like you really could.

Saving money seems hard at times. No matter what you make, it is good to put something aside. Even though you probably cannot put a whole lot up, something is better than nothing. Saving accounts are a good starter for beginners. Even if you do not make as much as you would like right now, still save something. Even if it is twenty dollars a week. A little will become a lot. We have heard many times that every penny counts. A penny makes a nickel; a nickel makes a dime and so forth. It may seem like things are not adding up if you are saving a small amount, but it adds up quickly.

If you are the type to spend your check as soon as you get it, you should consider getting direct deposit. You can contact the payroll department at your job and they can give you instructions concerning setting this up. By saving this way, you never even see the money, so it is less tempting. If you do decide to go this route, always check your check stub to make sure your money is right. In addition, you could let your spouse handle your check if they are responsible. When saving, it is good to set goals. Make your goal reachable. Do not start off with large goals.

Saving money is something that is easier said than done. There is more to it than spending less money. First you must decide, how much money will you save, where will you put it, and how can you make sure it stays there. Here is how to set realistic goals, keep your spending in check, and pay yourself first.

Some Simple Steps to Promote Saving

1. Always set saving goals. Short-term goals are easy to set and conquer pretty fast. If you wanted to save for a business start up, find out how much it costs; if you want to buy a house, determine how much of a down payment you will need. For long term goals, such as retirement, you'll need to do a lot more planning to figure out how much money you'll need to live comfortably. When saving long term, you'll also need to figure out how investments will help you achieve your goal.

2. Always set a time frame or deadlines. For example: "I want to be able to buy a house two years from today." Set a particular date for accomplishing shorter-term goals, and make sure the goal is attainable. If it is not attainable, you will just get discouraged.

3. Always calculate how much you will need to save per week, per month, or per paycheck to attain each of your savings goals. Most of the time, it is best to save the same amount each period. This is important because you will get in a rhythm and get use to saving without it being a strain. It is good to get the money deducted before you even see it.

4. Always keep good records of your expenses. What you save will fall between two things. This includes how much you make and how much you spend out. Obviously, you have more control over how much you spend. It is important to frugal to get ahead. Write down everything you spend your money on for the month to get track of expenses. Evaluate this and make adjustments when needed.

5. Always look for ways to trim your expenses. Take a good hard look at your spending records after a month or two have passed.

6. Always follow a budget. Once you have managed to balance your earnings with your savings goals and spending, write down a budget so you will know each month or each paycheck how much you can spend on any given thing or category of things.

7. Try not to use credit cards as less as possible. Pay for everything with cash or money orders if you can. Try not to use banks that charge fees for writing checks and using the ATM.

8. Open interest-bearing savings accounts. It is a lot easier to keep track of your savings if you have them separate from your spending money. You can also usually get better interest on money market accounts than checking accounts. Consider higher-interest options such as cd's and IRA's

9. Always know where your money is and how much you have. If you accidentally overdraw your bank account, you will incur hefty bank fees; worse yet, the place you paid with that check may slap a bounced check fee on top of that, and send the checks in again, resulting in second overdraft fee from the bank! So just a few cents missing to cover that check could result in over $100 in fees. To avoid that, you should always know how much you have got in your account(s), so you never cut a check for more than what you have.

10. Always pay yourself first. Saving should always be your priority, so do not just say that you will save whatever is left over at the end of the month. You can set up an automatic transfer from our checking account to your saving account.

GIVE BACK

YOU HAVE PROBABLY HEARD that it is better to give than to receive. This is not saying receiving is a bad thing, but giving is simply divine. This key pertains to the principle that if you give, you shall receive in return. This principle works! If you give, blessings will surely follow. Think about it as planting seeds. When someone plant seeds, it is understood that they expect a harvest. Just as with giving and receiving. When we give, we are setting ourselves up for blessings. Most of the time when you reap your harvest, it will be more than what you planted. God will honor this especially when we do it sincerely.

Giving attracts giving to come back to you. The good thing is, you can get more in return. Sometimes its tenfold, twenty fold, or more. This is better than the bank. If you desire more money, you should give money. If you desire more love, you should give love.

If you desire more appreciation, you should give appreciation. When we give, we receive. This is a mystery, but it works! You will become a human distribution center receiving and sending. Have you noticed that wealthy people give money away all the time? Think about the billions of dollars Bill Gates give away a year. Do you think he would do this if he thought he would not get it back? Wealthy people have mastered the keys to success and keep their focus on areas that give repeated returns. When we give our subconscious mind goes into a mode that feels like we have abundance even if we don't. When this occurs, we draw abundance to us, therefore reaping more. This goes back to reprogramming the mind. Remember that everything in the physical is birthed from the supernatural or subconscious mind. This is deep!

When giving, always do it willingly. Have you ever asked someone for something and they gave it to you reluctantly. Even though they gave it, you get the feeling that they really did not want to. Think about the times when you were growing up and you asked a sibling to share. When giving, we must give freely. God will honor this if when we do it with the right intentions. Some people give to others always expecting something in return. This is the wrong way to give. Of course, the principle is give and you shall receive, but give in the spirit of not looking for anything in return. It is that spirit that honors by giving back to you with interest. When we give in the right way, it can be life changing.

Giving does not always mean taking money out of your wallet. Giving could be as simple as sharing your time or information. It is easy to get sidetracked thinking that money is the only way to give. Many times, giving tough love is more valuable than giving money. The main thing is, train yourself to recognize opportunities to give or bless someone else. If everyone today had this attitude of helping others, the world would be a better place.

Giving helps keep us grounded. It provides a sense of responsibility and gratefulness to the success you have been allowed to achieve. When you are able to give, it makes you aware of where you have come from or where you could be. Sometimes people become successful and begin to look down on people in a status they once were in themselves. It is good to remain thankful as if you have not accomplished anything at all. Becoming high minded and puffed-up is a sign of decline in character away from true success.

Giving is the secret to keeping your money. Giving is the secret for receiving more money. Giving is the key to keeping money, success, health, love and happiness circulating in your life. There is a spiritual principle concerning give and it shall be given to you. This works! Again, giving is not all about money. My rewards have been greater when I have simply given a helping hand. Whether it is money or time, I am grateful to give. I have learned how to get my blessings. When I give, I am so grateful because I know I just received a blessing in two ways. One way is, I just helped someone else. The second way is, I just planted a seed to receive another blessing. I enjoy keeping my garden plentiful with seeds planted. I have an expectancy at all times because I have seeds planted. When harvest time comes, I expect to reap many benefits.

OVERVIEW

WHAT IS YOUR PURPOSE? Why are you here? What do you have to give to others? I have learned that everyone has something to give or contribute to the world. You have a lot to give. Your destiny is predetermined. Will you walk in your destiny? Will you take the keys to success and use the road map. Will you have an awakening moment and bring out the best in you. It is time! It is time to seize the moment in your life. Choose today to start your journey of success. It is time to get sick and tired of the same old results. It is time to take action! Surely, if you do the same old things, you will continue to get the same old results. Awaken the power within you and follow your dreams. If you are not living your dream, you are helping build someone else's dream. How long will you put off being a part of your own dream? Yes, there will be risks, but is there anything that does not have risks? Go to school, start your business, etc. What do you have to lose? You have your dreams and desires to gain. Success happens for others, so why not you? It is time for you to go beyond your fears. Fear is only a state of mind. If you never start at all, someone else surely will. If you give up, someone else will surely finish. Failure is not an option anymore. Block out the negative thoughts of giving up. Always take an active approach and never accept no for an answer. It is your time if you believe it is your time. It is definitely your life and your success is up to you. You do not get a practice life. Utilize your time wisely. Recognize and take advantage of every opportunity. Time waits on no man. Five minutes ago is already gone. Plan ahead now and make the right choices. It is up to you to decide what you want to do and achieve. Stop letting others decide what you want to do and achieve for you. From this day forward, be a part of your own life by utilizing research and always making informed decisions. Your life choices are simply your choices. Your state of life equals to the choices you make. Again, be a part of your own life by reprogramming your mind to a mind with a successful outlook. By reading this book, you have illustrated that you are seeking success or higher success. Success is yours just for the asking. Remind yourself each day that it is your dream, your goal, and finally your success.

SPECIAL THANKS

I THANK GOD FOR allowing me to complete this book to share general principles concerning success to my kids and anyone who desire to be successful. Special thanks to all of my family, business associates, employees, attorneys, accountant, church family, church affiliations, organizations, fans, and all the people I mentor. To Rose (wife) and to my mini-me Christina, I love you. Thanks for always lifting me up allowing me to share my time with others. To my son, C.J. you're going to do big things son, daddy love you. To my son Christian, you are a star and daddy love you big boy! Thanks Mom for always being supportive and a friend, I love you always. To my beloved father, your wisdom continues on today. I strive to be like you. Thanks to Queenie Williams, Angela Powe (Too Sweet), Gwen Johnson, Elder Jimmie Lee Williams Jr. (Bug) , Cassandra " Sand" Williams, Sharon Adams, Patricia Williams, Stephanie Sellers, Bishop Maurice Williams, Wycondia West, Derrick Williams. Rosie Smith "Ma" , Tekela Ely, Jerome Smith, Dr. Veronica Hudson, Marion Smith, Vanessa Henry, Bradley Smith, Carolyn Westry, Herman Smith, Kenneth Smith. All of my nieces, nephews, cousins, etc.

I thank all of my mentors: Thank you all for sharing your knowledge and wisdom. Truly, no one becomes successful alone. Thank you for making me seem smart. Thanks Billy Brown II. You have been a major influence on me. Your story is inspirational! You're my mentor for life. Thank you for being a part of my success team. Thank you Devin Nobles. You are a very smart businessman. Special thanks to Mr. Sam Parker and Carol Parker. I admire your wisdom! Thanks Larry Scott, Leanna Ragley, Pam Williams, Mamie Mackey, Theresa Nobles for always sharing and putting up with me bugging. You all are so bright. Thanks Carol Westry for being dependable, thank you always! Satish, thank you, thank you, thank you. Your knowledge is priceless. Butch Franklin, you are my investor for life. Thank you for taking me to another level. Thanks Mike Patrick for always sharing your wisdom. Thanks to everyone who has given me wisdom and sound advice over the years and even today.

Special thanks to Volunteers of America Southeast for believing in me and for a great business relationship. Thank you Dr. Deanna Ferguson, Dr. Wallace Davis, Jana Farley, Beverly Pickens, Michelle Vaughn, Joel Harvey, Cathy Flowers, RN Kathie, Carla, Charlotte, Quita, Fennie, Mary, Tasha, Meeka, Nycole, Africa, Rondi Wilkens. A very special thanks to Pastor Tecia and Rodney Chastang! I could never repay you for all I owe you both. I love you both forever and thank you for your leadership and guidance. I would not be where I am today without you! Thanks Pastor Curtis and Eva Reed, Karen Hammond, Mr. Donald Hammond, Melody and Joe Thompson, Mary Love, Dorothy Graham, Prentiss Graham, Linda Lopez, Lillian Knox, Anthony Knox, John Smith, Roy Smith. Alabama Providers of Mobile especially Gayle and Robert Brown, Denise Stallworth, Mellisa Ezell, Alabama Providers Statewide, Erica Deeds, Alysea Powell, Coronda Sims, Dominque Gibson, William Ely, Jarnisha "Shay" Young, Michelle Holloway and Family, Providence Family Physicians Dr. Alan Sherman, Deborah Hyatt, Andrea, and the rest of the crew. Also thanks to M.A.R.C., Independent Learning Center, Michael Davis, Brandy Goodson, Resources for Independence, American Red Cross, Alta Pointe Health Systems, Girls Scouts International, Shasta's World, My Sister Keepers 7, Mini Warehouse (Dawn Reese), Mayor Ron Davis (Prichard, AL), Troy Epiphriam, City Counsel, late Mayor Ken Williams (Saraland), Dr. Rubenstein Mayor Saraland, Mayor Sam Jones (Mobile, AL), and all business affiliations. Alta Pointe 310 Board, especially Rose Skanes, Theresa Mc Millian, Johnice Edwards, Shaloundra Holmes, Shirley Kidd, Natasha Taylor and the rest of the crew. DMH, especially Jerrilyn London, Mickey Groggel, Lori Leathers, Shirley Patterson, Zina May, Jean Long, Steve Lloyd, Jane Johnston, Beth Rodgers, James Packer, Ana Sawyer, Celestine Chappell, John Williams, Cathy Smith, Dr. Todd Luellen, Bradley Lamey, Miranda Warner, David Zizkind, Winifred Blackledge, Yolanda Thomas, Kendra Butler, Donna Buckley, Clara Mc Brayer, Bob Cunningham, Certification, Eight Mile Nursing Home, and Springhill Memorial Hospital, Mobile County Sheriff's Department, Mobile County Metro Jail, City of Mobile, City of Prichard, City of Saraland, Saraland Toastmasters, Toastmasters International, Shasta's World, JLW Place Inc., J. Rodgers Barbecue, Living Water Apostolic, Freewill Pentecostal, High Point Baptist Church, Chunchula Apostolic, Saraland Apostolic, Word of Life, Pastor Clyde Maye, Kushla AME Church, all Church of God Pentecostal Inc., Dauphin Way Baptist Church, Fountain of Life, Evangel Christian School, Church of God in Christ International, Alabama Family, Houston Texas Family, Mississippi Family, Florida Family, California Family, New York City Family, New Jersey Family, Italy Family. If I forgot your name or company, I apologize and thank you now.